BEHIND THE BULLET POINTS

THE SURPRISING SECRETS OF POWERFUL
PRESENTATIONS

DON E. DESCY, PH.D.

Bay View Editions
Professional Series
Fennbrook Media Group (USA), Ltd.

3 5 7 9 10 8 6 4 2
Copyright © 2021 by Don E. Descy
All rights reserved.

Printed in the United States of America
Editing, interior design and cover design: Paul Hawkins, Berlin, Germany

For more information about special discounts for bulk purchases, please
contact
Fennbrook Media Group Sales at 507-351-2528.

ISBN: 978-0-9994829-0-2

CONTENTS

To my wife, Glenna,
who has been with me all the way.

FOREWORD

When I first started presenting, I was petrified to speak in front of an audience. I was terrified that I would become tongue-tied or forget what I wanted to say. I was mortified by the thought of making a total fool of myself. However, after a relatively short time I came up with techniques and strategies that actually made presenting in front of an in-person or virtual group a rewarding experience both for me and for my audience.

The one thing I ask is that you forget everything you have ever been taught, learned, or read about presenting. Have you taken a speech class? Forget about it. Have you been reading any of the scores of other books professing to tell you how to be a great presenter? Forget about them. Ditto all of those websites you have looked at. Ditto what other people have said to you. Ditto what you think presenting should be. Wipe your mind clean. Got that?

PoweredPointer 1: Forget everything you have ever been taught, read, heard, or learned about presenting

CHAPTER 1

SO YOU HAVE TO GIVE A PRESENTATION

There are two things that professional presentation and speech gurus will tell you to do. The first is to commit to memory almost everything you want to say. The second is that you *should*, or others even say *must*, be yourself. I don't believe that you have to do either of these. As a matter of fact, I believe that if you follow this advice, it will actually make your presenting more difficult and anxiety producing.

You don't have to write out your presentation word for word and then commit to memory. However, you do need to practice your presentation over and over again. You don't even have to write what you want to say on note cards. And quite frankly, I have rarely seen a presenter 'be themselves'. Being yourself might work in some cases but not in very many. How can you be yourself if you have to craft your presentation and yourself to your specific audience? I am sure that your speech teacher or these presentation gurus have also told you how to design your PowerPoint slides, told you to always talk directly to your audience, and told you to limit your movements during your presentation. Forget about these things also! I truly believe that if you follow my advice, you will soon be well on your way to becoming a power presenter: one who gets their message across effectively and efficiently with control, confidence and a minimum of anxiety.

First, let me tell you a little story. It is about me. I have always been a quiet individual. (That is an understatement at best.) I, probably like you, had a fear of presenting before a group. Yet for some reason I ended up in front of a classroom. I wanted to make a little more money so I quit my job and went back to school. I finally ended my studies with a 'terminal degree'. Now I *had* to find a job. I wanted to put my degree to work and was lucky enough to find a position teaching at a university. I liked teaching and doing research but unfortunately they were not heavily emphasized in our department. Our department did heavily emphasize service. Service in our department meant being involved in state, national, and sometimes even international professional organizations.

In our department, 'involvement' meant 'presenting'… presenting…and more presenting. This was definitely something I did not want to do. I did not want to talk in front of a group. They didn't tell me about this requirement before I signed on the dotted line! I had no choice now though. I would not be tenured for at least three years. I had my job cut out for me.

Well, present I did. First I presented with my boss and a few other people, and as time progressed I presented by myself. I even learned (over time) to be a good (well really good) presenter. In a little more time I became a real power presenter! People would actually come around to see my presentations just to see me. I had fun. They seemed to enjoy it. And they said that they learned a great deal. Don't laugh —*I* had a following! My own groupies! I guess that is called *positive reinforcement!* And that positive reinforcement helped me actually enjoy presenting.

Don't get me wrong. I still had the jitters for 24 to 48 hours before *each and every* presentation. Almost all presenters have the jitters before they present. I did hit my presentations running (but scared), and at the end I was really pleased with the results. By the time I retired I had done about 500 presentations in-person and virtually in the US, Canada, Europe, and Asia. As I said, I did have the jitters (and more) before every—every—presentation I made (again: *we all have the jitters before we go 'on stage'*) but I knew what to do, and I had confidence that I could do it. And remember, this from a person who still does not like to be pointed out in a group. I skipped out of several awards ceremonies towards the end of my career because my professional organization was presenting something to me... and when I retired, I refused all parties and skipped the last few department and university meetings for the same reason.

I should stop here for a moment to mention a few things. The reason you should go all-out to be a super presenter is not to be popular or have 'groupies'. It is to have people trust you, to have people believe what you are saying, and more importantly, to be able to get your information across to them in an effective and efficient manner. In my case, and perhaps in yours as well, it also helped me keep my job! It does help if your audience (and your cohorts and boss) likes you and enjoys your presentations. But again: trust, believability, and getting your information across to your audience is the bottom line.

Let me reemphasize PoweredPointer 1: *Forget everything you have ever read, heard, or learned about presenting.* Just wipe your mind clean and listen, hear, and read what I have to say. Think about the words and the ideas in this book. What I will tell you here will make sense and if you follow my advice I can just about guarantee that your presentations will get your points across, be enjoyed by the audience and yourself, and best of all, be stress free. Ready? Let's go!

CHAPTER 2

LET'S TALK ABOUT YOU

Before I sat down to write this book, I read countless books on public speaking and presentation skills to see what other authors had to say on the subject. I did not want to reinvent the wheel. Most of the books said that if you follow what the author said in their particular book, you would become a great public speaker. Hmm, didn't you just read that a few minutes ago? I am 100% sure that all the other authors also think the same way about their books. Anyone who decides to write a self-help book on any subject would say that you would learn great ideas from their book, and I am sure that each and every author believes it too. *"Buy my book, read my book, and it's a crap shoot whether or not it will do you any good"* probably would not look good on a back cover. To be honest, if I believed that those other authors could really help you, I would not be writing this book. Although many of those other books have some useful information in them, much of what they say is not helpful and, worse than that, may even decrease your ability to feel comfortable as you give your presentation or participate in a virtual meeting. Or worse yet, it could even decrease your ability to get your message across. After all, getting your message across efficiently (with a minimum of jitters) is what this book is all about. Just about every book I have ever read on the topic of public speaking has said: 'Be yourself.' I will tell you what I think about this right from the get-go: *DON'T BE YOURSELF!*

You are an actor on a stage

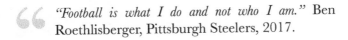

> *"Football is what I do and not who I am."* Ben Roethlisberger, Pittsburgh Steelers, 2017.

It is not about you! *You* are not the most important entity-thing-being in the room. Your *message* is the most important entity-thing-being. You are number two. You are the medium that transmits your message. You are important because you have to be configured in such a way as to enhance and not detract from your message. That's right: *you have to be configured.* And, if you have to be configured or changed to more efficiently get your message across, you will not be yourself. You will be a 'configured' you. This chapter is centered on making you more 'configured'. Remember my words: *Don't be yourself.*

PoweredPointer 2: Don't be yourself

The most important point to remember at all times is that you are an actor on a stage. Just like an actor, your job is to get the message across. Your only job is to get the message across.

Who or what you are is not important—unless you are some great and famous person in your field—but even then, remember, you are an actor on a stage. You (the real you) are not important. *You have to be a person your audience can identify with.* You have to play to your audience to get your message across just as an actor plays to his audience to get his message or emotions across. Don't worry, it is easier than it sounds. (So much for the 'be yourself' crowd!)

PoweredPointer 3: Play to your audience

Just being an actor is not enough

How many times have you been brought to tears, fits of laughter, or been frightened out of your wits from watching an actor in a movie?

Tears, laughter or fear were the emotions that the actor wanted to get across to you. The actor—the person on the movie set—is the person who gave this emotion wings and transmitted it to your brain. There is someone who is even more important in attendance and who is probably the most important person on the set. That person is the director. The director choreographs the whole scene.

 "The director is the person who sets the tone of the movie and interprets the script as he sees it... He instructs the actors on how to say their lines, their facial expressions and tone. Virtually anything that happens on a movie set is subject to the approval of the director." (Lee, 2006).

The actor gets the message and emotions across to the audience, but the director is really the one in the background playing the actor like a puppet. The director tells the actor how to look, move, gesture, and deliver their lines. Just like an actor, a director can make or break a scene.

Do you see a potential problem here?

There is no director to tell you what to do when you are presenting. There is one director on the scene though: *you!* You are the actor *and* the director! So what can you do?

One of the key items you must always complete before any presentation is an audience analysis. To play to a group of people, you really have to know as much about them as possible. We will spend a whole chapter on this: Chapter 4: Know your audience. You will also find *PoweredGuide 1: Audience analysis* in Appendix 2 at the end of this book.

You should also carry out at least one full dress rehearsal of your presentation in front of an audience of (honest) friends so they can give you pointers—help *direct* you as it were. Remember, though, to share what you found in your audience analysis with them so they will know something about whom you will be presenting to and what to look for as you present. *PoweredGuide 9: Rehearsal Checklist and Comments* in Appendix 2 should be very useful for this exercise. You should also tape the rehearsal so you can review everything about how and what you are presenting so you can also give yourself pointers! Most of us are harder on ourselves than on others and may see some things that our rehearsal reviewers might gloss over or miss. Most of us miss things or take things for granted as we review our presentation, hence the rehearsal reviewers. As the actor and director, you have to design your own scene and direct what your audience will see, hear, and feel. Everything you do is important. Even the little things!

 "Design works not because people understand or even appreciate it but because it works subliminally. Just like background music in a store. Nobody would admit to being influenced by it, but it generates a mood, whether we listen consciously or not." (Medium, 2015).

The above quotation might be enough to send some of you to "I'll never present island." But really, that is the key: everything you do during your presentation, speech or keynote be it in-person or virtual will directly affect its outcome. Don't worry; I will cover everything you need to know in the following pages. By the end of this book you will be confident to be in charge and be able to carry your 'show'!

Ronald Reagan once said:

"… An actor knows two important things—to be honest in what he's doing and to be in touch with the audience." (Cannon, 2000).

Notice that President Reagan did not say "Be yourself…"

PoweredPointer 4: Audience members make up their minds about you virtually as soon as they see you

You have to hit the ground running

Websites are lucky. Research has shown that a typical website has seven seconds to establish credibility, trust, and value (CreativeMMS, 2012).

A (whole!) seven seconds. Why do I say websites are lucky?

 "According to published research, people form an opinion on whether they can trust you in one tenth of a second." (Ellett, 2010).

One tenth of a second.

We have reached one of the most important points in this book. You don't have seven seconds to influence your audience. Let's face it, if your audience does not trust you, or form a positive opinion of you (research seems to say in an instant), you may have lost the game before you even open your mouth. Notice I said *before*. How your audience responds to you, how they perceive you, how they respond to what you are going to say, all starts in the fraction of a second when they see you as they enter the room. *Before* you have started your 'presentation'. *Before* you have even opened your mouth. Perhaps even *before* you have even become aware that someone is in the room. You are 'presenting' from the moment another person enters your presentation room. Their perception of trust and believability in you and in your presentation begins instantly. *Unless your audience has a basic trust in you, they probably won't believe you.*

Slowly count to five as you to take a deep breath…and now exhale to a count of five. I have you covered!

CHAPTER 3

FIRST THEY HAVE TO TRUST YOU

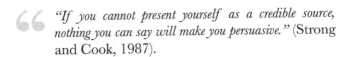 *"If you cannot present yourself as a credible source, nothing you can say will make you persuasive."* (Strong and Cook, 1987).

PoweredPointer 5: They have to trust you to believe you

Hmm. According to Michael Hyatt (Hyatt, n.d.), a New York Times best-selling author on salesmanship, "Having a great product is not enough." Hyatt also says that "(Trust) takes months—sometimes years—to build." Yes, he is talking about salespeople and not presenters. You do have a product—your presentation—that you hope to sell to your audience. I am sure you can spot a problem here. You don't have months or years. You have seconds and minutes—well, really you only have seconds. So what do you do?

Time to check some helpful research

In the 1960s Dr. Albert Mehrabian, a professor at UCLA, conducted a series of research studies to try to determine how words and/or body language (movement, facial expression, word tone, etc.) communicated a speaker's feelings and attitudes. Interestingly (and of statistical significance), his research revealed that the speaker's tone of voice was far more important in judging a speaker's true feelings on a subject than what he actually said about the subject. In further research, facial expressions were tested. Facial expressions seemed to be another key factor in influencing a subject's perception of the speaker.

Based on his research, Mehrabian stated that trust and believability could be separated into three components: How you *look*, how you sound (your *voice*), and finally, what you are saying (your actual *words*) (Mehrabian, 1971; 1980).

Mehrabian broke it down this way:

- Body language (how you look): 55%
- How you sound (voice): 38%
- What you are saying (your words): 7%

In the 2005 movie *Hitch*, Will Smith played the role of a 'dating doctor' who helped men win the women of their dreams. One of his most important lines was *"60% of all human communication is nonverbal body language; 30% is your tone, so that means 90% of what you're saying ain't coming out of your mouth."* (Sarkis, 2011).

The percentages may vary, but I believe that the essence of Mehrabian's research is accurate. As you read the following, you will note that I have reinterpreted his three components—with a bit of license—to meet my own needs. Though many others agree with my interpretation (see for example Devito, 1999), there are still others who believe that this is not what Mehrabian's research is saying (see Braithwaite, 2007 or Mitchell, n.d.). Still, research has shown that nonverbal cues more heavily influence first impressions than verbal cues. Specifically, nonverbal cues can be over four times more powerful at creating a first impression than anything you say (Goman, 2011). When verbal and nonverbal signals contradict each other, your audience members are up to five times more likely to believe your nonverbal cues (Argyle et al., 1971)!

PoweredPointer 6: First impressions are lasting impressions

"First impressions are lasting impressions…" (Smith and Mackie, 2007).

As indicated earlier, people judge you the moment they see you.

"It takes just one tenth of a second for us to judge someone and make our first impression." (Willis and Todorov, 2006).

When asked how long it takes for executives and managers (at a job interview) to judge your look and appearance, style expert Daisy Lewellyn says *"…immediately"* (Doyno, 2013).

Research has shown that we subconsciously perceive something, comprehend what it is, and decide whether we like it or not in a matter of milliseconds (Goleman, 2005). Note the word 'subconsciously' in that sentence. When you couple this with the fact that it is difficult for people to separate the message from the source (Strong and Cook, 1987), it is easy to understand the importance of being an authoritative source from the very moment an audience member enters your room.

"But I haven't even opened my mouth yet!"

I hope that you are beginning to understand why I still think we should keep Mehrabian's work uppermost in our minds since we are interested in getting people to trust us and believe in us as early as possible. The audience will make a lot of subconscious decisions about you and about your presentation before you even have a chance to open your mouth.

Now that I have put you at ease (*yeah, right*), let's look at how we might get the audience to form a good first impression of you. Luckily, it is not nearly as difficult as you might imagine. Think about the research: We assist our audience in the creation of a good first impression by controlling how we look and the body language we use.

PoweredPointer 7: Body language and your look – 55%

I would suspect that the very first thing audience members will see when they look at you is, well...you. They see how you look and how you dress. They will start to subconsciously interpret your body language at about the same time. You are onstage the moment an audience member enters the room. Luckily you have the time and the tools to prepare a good first impression beforehand when you are not under any pressure, before you enter the room and before your grand opening. Let us imagine at this time that you have researched your audience and know what to expect, and more importantly you have a good idea about what they expect. We will discuss how to research your audience, their likes and dislikes, and prepare for your presentation accordingly in a later chapter.

Dress for success

For now, let us say that you have researched your audience and know who they are and what they like. Perhaps they are teachers, lawyers, engineers, plumbers, parents and friends of the graduates, etc. There are several very important reasons why you have to know as much as possible about your audience. One is that it is vitally important that you dress appropriately for each group. You should know how *they* dress at meetings, at work, and in public. You want to mimic this. The 'way cool' college professor type who comes to class dressed in jeans and a *Che Guevara* T-shirt may actually be OK in certain situations, although I doubt it. I should have said that you should *almost* mimic your audience; you should dress one step above them. This shows respect for your audience and sets you up as a professional on their level...or slightly above. You are 'OK'. They can identify with you. You are one of them. Dressing up also helps you get into character. (You are an actor, remember?) And it also shows your audience that you care.

PoweredPointer 8: Dress one step above your audience

How you dress is one of the most important parts of how you look. You may not have control over your skin texture, body type, or general physical appearance, but you do have control over how you dress. Proper dress for the audience is about getting into character, and getting across to your audience, however subconsciously it may be, that you respect them. This actually increases their confidence and acceptance in what you are saying. Personally, I have a closet full of suits and sports coats. While they are all 'nice' (well, perhaps not all of them!), I have one really, really nice suit. It is made of black Italian wool and it has ever-so-faint thin blue pin stripes. I wear this suit when I have to present in front of higher-level business people (or New Yorkers). It would look really out of place at my professional association's conference though. For them, I wear a nice suit or a nice shirt, pants, tie (usually), and a sports coat. When I present, I rarely go below nice pants, a button-down shirt, and a tie. Well, perhaps no tie if there is no air conditioning. Oh, and once at Disney I did come out with mouse ears.

A female colleague of mine holds a very important position in a prestigious higher-learning institution. Through all of the years I've known her, I've never seen her dress unprofessionally and I have never (ever) seen her not carry a leather portfolio or a brief case. She once told me that she always carries this to 'look the part'. (At first I thought that she was joking.) She also takes multiple sets of clothing to conferences and may wear several outfits during the day depending on where she will be and what she will be doing. She has a matching watch for each outfit! All of this must be working. Her salary and benefits are worth well into six figures not to mention her other perks! She also travels with one of those adjustable light make-up mirrors and a set of make-up that allows her to match her make-up to the lighting and time of day. OK, OK, I know what you are thinking… (But…. six figures +…and that was way back in 2014!)

Margaret Thatcher (former Prime Minister of the United Kingdom from 1979 to 1990) used to carry thick, expensive black handbags as a symbol of her strength. She would carry documents in them that she would pull out to read quotations from at interviews (Dunbar, 2011).

Dress conservatively. Women (and men) should not wear flashy jewelry. You don't want to show off tattoos (unless your presentation is to a motor cycle club meeting) and—*many people don't like it when I say this*—don't show any affiliation except with the group you are talking to.

What do I mean by not showing affiliation? Of course you won't wear a campaign button during an election year (I hope), but you also should not wear anything that might carry a religious connotation other than a small symbol on a necklace. (That is unless you are a rabbi, pastor or nun, or have to wear it for other religious reasons.) Also, don't wear outfits that will draw attention to your ethnicity or country of origin. No lederhosen or dashiki shirts, please!

Several years ago I said this at one presentation and elicited a really dirty look and a not so under-breath "racist!" comment from a minority member in the audience. Unfortunately, people have their own sets of stereotypes and prejudices and we don't want to play into their baggage. Berklee College of Music voice professor and New Bedford (MA) jazz vocalist Armsted Christian emphasized this when he was discussing voice communications (honestly!). Professor Christian simply stated that "it's important that your message not be defeated by the color of your instrument." (Marean, 2009).

How you speak is very important

PoweredPointer 9: You must sound the part

How you sound also plays an important role in your trust and believability: 38% according to Mehrabian (1971). We may not think that we have much control over how the words sound as they come out of our mouths, but we do. Actors have voice coaches. Most of us don't. We still have to sound honest, we still have to sound sincere, and we still have to sound authentic. When we practice our presentations we not only have to commit the general content to memory (notice I am saying 'general' content and not 'memorize your presentation word for word'—more on that later), but we also have to practice how we are going to say the words. "Voice can convey things that words don't," says Morgan James (Mwalim) Peters, a spoken-word artist and English professor at the University of Massachusetts at Dartmouth (Marean, 2009). Like all actors on a stage, your voice (and stage presence) is one of the most important tools of your trade. With the introduction of talkies (motion pictures with sound), the fame and careers of many big-name silent film stars ended abruptly because of their disappointing voices (Iveson, 2012). The famous 1952 movie *Singing in the Rain* starring Gene Kelly, Donald O'Connor, and Debbie Reynolds dealt with the problem of a silent film actor with a high, funny voice trying to make the transition to sound motion pictures. You do not want this to happen to you! (I guess that is a bit overly dramatic, but I think you get my point.) Let's go over a few tricks that should help you.

One of the most important components of your voice is its pitch. Pitch has to do with the actual frequency a sound is composed of. A sound can have a high frequency or pitch (think of a mouse squeak) in one direction or a low frequency or pitch (think someone singing base) in the other direction. Pitch is the result of the vibration of the vocal cords. Generally speaking, both males and females find lower-pitched voices more attractive.

A study from Duke University found that men with deeper voices are more successful and also make about $187,000 *a year* more than higher-pitched men (Adams, 2013). (Note that was in 2013 dollars!) Other studies have found that men with lower-pitched voices win more elections, are more desirable to women, mate more frequently, and father more children (Chang, 2013; Mouland, 2010). At which point during my presentation I would turn slightly away from the audience, look back at them over my shoulder, lower my head a bit and slowly say—in my most sexy, throaty (and severely campy), low dramatic voice, "Isn't that (pause) true, ladies?" as I raised an eyebrow towards the audience.

And ladies, it is important that you have a relatively low pitch—but not too low—with a wider acoustic range and a more Marilyn Monroe-like *breathy* voice. (See for example the 1953 movie *Gentleman Prefer Blondes*, staring Marilyn Monroe and Tommy Noonan. I should warn you that this video is far from present-day PC.) Many female and male lawyers have voice therapy and even former Prime Minister Margaret Thatcher, who we mentioned earlier, took speech lessons at the Royal National Theatre to give her a calm, authoritative voice with a lower pitch. Before her speech lessons, her critics complained that she had a very shrill voice. "Soon the hectoring tones of the housewife gave way to softer notes and a smoothness that seldom cracked except under extreme provocation on the floor of the House of Commons," wrote her biographer and close friend Charles Moore (Dunbar, 2011).

Hillary Clinton, the first female United States presidential candidate was known as 'shrill-ary" ever since she was Arkansas's first lady. Bob Woodward lamented that "she shouts, there's something unrelaxed about the way she's communicating," and former RNC chair Michael Steele said she was "going up every octave with every word." There are actually several articles in print asking the question, "Would you really like Hillary more if she sounded different?" (Khazan, 2016).

So, how do you change your pitch? How do you deepen your voice? One way is to talk to yourself! Try it right now. Say "Bum, bum, bum…" and keep on repeating these words using a deeper and deeper voice until you have 'bottomed out'. Keep repeating the words as low as you can go for five repetitions. Just keep on practicing this whenever you get a chance, *especially before your presentation.* This should help 99% of you. The other 1% may want to seek professional help.

Do professionals really do all this vocal stuff? When I first wrote this part of the book, I was recuperating from a foot operation I had several weeks earlier. I was on the couch 24 hours a day, so I was not very tired at night. One night—at 12:02 am—I turned on the radio and dial twisted to a distant radio station. The on-air personality was a semi-well-known female comedian. Just after I turned it on, the young man who read the traffic report came into the studio. The host said that she was surprised that the traffic reporter was coming in to talk with her. She then said that before midnight she had been in the studio doing her vocal exercises when the traffic reporter walked in, and hearing what was happening, made a hasty retreat. At this point in the narration the traffic reporter chimed in and asked the on-air personality what she would have done if she had opened a door to a studio and found someone sitting inside repeating "bum, bum, bum" in a low voice over and over again! (OK, it was funnier at midnight, but it does add at least some credibility to the point I am trying to make!)

PoweredPointer 10: Practice your bums!

Remember to speak slowly. As we increase our speed, our pitch tends to rise. We are also easier to understand and follow if we speak slowly. Remember, your audience is digesting what you are saying and is probably taking notes. Conversational speech should be about 100 to 125 words per minute. I have no idea how fast that is. There are probably *YouTube* videos out there of people speaking at that rate. But again, your audience will be taking notes and listening (intently). So take it easy and pause after you make a point. Don't forget to add some short, silent moments to give your audience a chance to mull over what you have just said. One public speaking coach actually says that a presenter should wait three fast beats between sentences. Mmm, I think that adding these pauses might sound a bit mechanical though...just remember to pause if audience members are busy taking notes and/or thinking or even looking confused. It is always a good idea to keep an eye on your audience for feedback on how you and they are doing as you go along.

How can we tell how fast we are speaking? Sometimes it is easy, but most times it is not. In the heat of the moment we are so excited, perhaps a bit scared, that we may not know that we are racing through our presentation. Stressful situations tend to increase our rate of speaking. We don't always notice that we are talking fast. Many times, we think that we are talking at a normal pace and, even though it took a tight hour to go over the presentation in an empty room, we find that we are left standing in front of the audience with nothing more to say with 10 minutes left to fill. We look blankly at the audience. They look blankly back at us. We smile. They smile. This could get a bit awkward, unless you have a back-up strategy in your pocket.

At this point, it might be a good idea to ask for questions from the audience. There is, of course, an art to asking and answering questions (I will cover audience questions and answers later.) This is where recording yourself during more than one of your (many) rehearsals can be helpful. Recording rehearsals should help you with timing and pacing your voice along with identifying places to insert any pauses that may be necessary. There is nothing like real audience feedback though.

Here are a few ways to tell if you are speaking too fast. First, notice your breathing. Is it shallow? Are you breathing from the top of your lungs? If you are breathing correctly, you will be breathing from the lower part of your lungs: slowly and deeply. Yes, I know, how can you tell how your lungs are doing when your heart might be racing? Check the tension in your jaw. Does it feel tight as you talk? Try to relax your jaw and open your mouth wider. Enunciate your words. Good enunciation is a complete facial workout. Proper enunciation usually requires that your lips, mouth, tongue, and jaw are moving. And finally, pay more attention to your audience and not to your content. By the time you stand up in front of the group, you know what you are going to say, and since I told you earlier—and will discuss later—that you should not memorize your presentation, you will not have to worry about losing your place. That is why we have bullets on note cards and/or PowerPoint bullets on the screen.

PoweredPointer 11: Your words are important

Mehrabian says that your actual words add only about 7% to your trust and believability. I know that this seems really low. It is. But I guess with all this talk of 'fake news' going on these days, it is easier to see that words in and of themselves may or may not be enough. I am at a small disadvantage. Right now I am not 'presenting' you the information in the book. But rather you are reading my 'printed presentation'. I do hope that you trust me and believe what I am writing... at least more than 7%! But what does Mehrabian mean when he says *words?* He is not saying just the words as on this printed page. Rather Mehrabian means *words* as a part of the whole presentation package: *look, sound, words.* Since this 'printed' presentation is just words, their and my believability should be a great deal higher... I hope.

Again, you should make every effort to record your practice runs and first 'public' presentations. You should (of course) listen to how you are enunciating your words. You should also be on the lookout for your use of fillers. Fillers are words like 'OK?', 'uh', 'you know', 'right?', etc. Fillers can (and do) distract from your message and can actually be very irritating to your listeners. Unfortunately, many of us have no idea that we are doing it. I am sure that we have all sat through presentations where the presenter subconsciously has added fillers. In some situations bored audience members have been known to put a little hatch mark on their papers each time a presenter uses a particular filler. I have seen this happen several times as I have sat through presentations. I guess I was watching the audience more than the presenter!

Would you like to be thought of as tiring, boring, and hatch marked, or even untrustworthy? This is what will happen if you speak in a monotone. It is as simple as that. Add expression to your voice. Remember, you are an actor on a stage. Do what it takes vocally to get your point across. Have a little fun…don't be embarrassed; you may never see these people again! Your audience will be more receptive and interested in what you are saying if you are dynamic. Just don't go overboard! Watch how your audience responds to your presentation. Audience smiles and nods will be great feedback. So will yawns and fidgeting and side conversations and comments to their neighbors.

PoweredPointer 12: Practice, practice, practice your timing and delivery

BTW FWIW RTFM (IANAL)*

Pick your words carefully. Your words must match your audience. Unless you know for a fact that everyone is on the same page, be careful how you use your words. Jargon, acronyms, buzzwords, and slang can be real minefields. Many times when I use subject specific jargon for the first time I stop to tell the audience what I mean, or after explaining something I may go the other way and stop and say, "Many of us would call this *(insert jargon word/phrase.)*" It is a good idea to always define an acronym the first time you use it. If there is an extended period of time before you use it again—in the closing perhaps—define it again at that time. Buzzwords and slang are really informal and trendy and may even sound pretentious. It is best to avoid buzzwords and slang in your presentations if at all possible. After listening to a presentation a few years back, my friend turned to me and said, "Shorthand can shortchange listeners." I looked around at some of the audience members' faces and realized how true that is. *By the way, for what it's worth read the fine manual. (I am not a lawyer.)

You are the U in humor

Over the years I am sure that you have been told or heard a great deal about humor in speeches and presentations. In several of the books on presenting that I have read, the comments were usually not to use humor in your presentation at all. I tend to disagree. Humor will give your presentation a lift, make your presentation more memorable, relax your audience, and—really important here—help you to relax. It will also give you an idea about how closely your audience is listening to you! People don't expect you to be a comedian. I am sure that you don't think of yourself as one. If you do, you may be in the wrong business. Being a comedian among friends or even in a comedy club is a whole different ball game. This is a presentation, not a comedy show. But the right amount of humor at exactly the right moments can dramatically increase the success of the presentation. In some of my repeat presentations, I would use the same humorous moment at the same place time after time, year after year. Remember a humorous moment might be just that. It does not have to be something spoken but could be just a look or a gesture. Remember what I said earlier about my actions when I talk about men with deep voices?

I once saw a video of an old-time comedian named Jack Benny doing a skit. (I know, many of you are saying, or at least thinking: *"Jack who?"*.) At one point, he stopped, folded his arms and just looked deadpan at the audience. The audience roared. This was one of Jack's signature gestures and has become known as the 'Jack Benny Pause'. As a matter of fact, in the opening credits for his later TV shows the title was on the left portion of the screen and a pencil sketch of Jack in his signature 'pause' was on the right portion of the screen. It was said that his biggest laughs came in the spaces between gags—not necessarily from the gag itself but from the mannerisms he employed right afterwards. If you have never seen Jack Benny perform, I am sure you can find a YouTube video showing him in action.

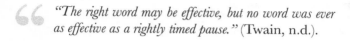

"The right word may be effective, but no word was ever as effective as a rightly timed pause." (Twain, n.d.).

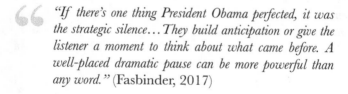

"If there's one thing President Obama perfected, it was the strategic silence…They build anticipation or give the listener a moment to think about what came before. A well-placed dramatic pause can be more powerful than any word." (Fasbinder, 2017)

PoweredPointer 13: Properly placed pauses punctuate perfectly planned presentations

The time you take going over the material before you actually have an audience in front of you can make the difference between a successful and an unsuccessful (or should we say not as successful) presentation. Humor comes in the rewrite though. We usually don't put it in the presentation as we write it. You may have an idea about a humorous incident as you prepare your first draft. In that case, jot it down separately. You can always add some humor later as you polish your presentation. In later rehearsals you might decide that the humor should be removed because it is not funny or does not support your point. Sometimes humor just comes to you during a presentation. You might just ad lib it during a presentation, although this is generally not a good idea if you are new to presenting. You really don't want anything that will break the flow of the presentation, and bad or misplaced humor can do just that. At first you may not put a lot of humor in your presentations, but with a little luck, you will develop this skill over time.

PoweredPointer 14: Humor can help your audience connect to you and your message

There are a few points to remember about humor:

Make it relevant

Humor must fit into the context of the presentation. It should help you to advance your objectives. Again, my action after I talk about deep voices in males should help place my point in their memory. Don't start with a joke for the sake of a joke. It should be a relevant starting point for your presentation.

Humor should be easy for your audience to connect with

We will talk about defining your audience a bit later. Let us just say that you have to know who your audience is. My peers at a professional meeting would probably connect with various humorous events quite differently than they would at a presentation on a similar topic to library media specialists or business people. Humor is the means to the end, not the end in itself. At one point in a presentation on Internet credibility I held up a *Wall Street Journal* (which just 'happened' to be folded on a table near me). I unfolded the paper and held the front page towards the audience and commented that most people generally trust what they read in a national newspaper. Heads nodded. At this point I casually dropped the *Wall Street Journal* to reveal a copy of the *Weekly World News – The World's*

Only Reliable News (It did cease printed publication but is now available online by subscription!). The headline on the one I used stated: "HILLARY CLINTON ADOPTS ALIEN BABY." A picture of Hillary Clinton holding a space alien baby filled the right half of the page. I did not say a word but just hesitated for a few seconds, put the papers on the desk and went right on with my presentation.

(©1993, Weekly World News. *Used with permission.)*

It is best to direct humor towards yourself

Jack Benny often gave the best lines to his supporting cast, and his Jack Benny 'pause' would be one of confusion, astonishment, anger, helplessness, etc. I have used this 'pause' several times between when I have stated something that did not seem to make sense and my explanation of why I said it. This self-deprecating humor hurts no one and helps the audience connect with you. We have all had embarrassing or self-deprecating moments. Almost a hundred years ago (1932) Benny made his radio debut. His opening line was "This is Jack Benny talking,"—(followed by a pause)—his next line was: "Who cares?" Again, it is always best to direct humor towards yourself. Remember, you are an actor on a stage. It is not about you. It is about your information. Don't be so stuck on yourself that you are afraid to show vulnerability.

Go out of your way to avoid offensive humor

There should be no reason for me to even have to say this. Don't ever use off-color, racist, sexist or ethnic humor. We should also add political to that list. Also avoid sarcasm. If in doubt, leave it out.

Don't force humor

Adding humor for the sake of humor can be disastrous. Humor can be an anecdote (a story or tale), a quote, an analogy ("I feel like…"), or an aside (a short comment or digression). Not everyone can tell a joke. A strong sense of timing is needed. If you don't think you have it, perhaps you could start with baby steps. Sometimes it is easier to start with a quote, anecdote, analogy, or an aside.

Got all of that? Good. We will get back to some of these points later. But now, on to this thing about knowing your audience.

CHAPTER 4

KNOW YOUR AUDIENCE

O K, let's say that you have been asked to give a presentation to a group or a business meeting. (You may have been *told* that you *have* to give one. That is what happened to me!) What should you do even before you start thinking about what you are going to say? What are you going to ask even if you have a previous presentation 'on the shelf' that you think you can use? First, you should find out as much as you can about who you will be presenting to—your audience. I cannot stress enough how important this is.

PoweredPointer 15: Know your audience

Here are two examples from my life that will emphasize both sides of this.

Yes, yes, yes! (Knowing your audience): In my early career, I did a presentation at my national professional technology organization. It was designed and given to the K-12 subgroup. Thankfully, the presentation was well received. My new colleague (the one with the briefcase/portfolio I mentioned earlier) was in the audience. A few months later she called me and asked me if I could come over to her university to give that presentation at one of their yearly conferences. She said that it would fit in perfectly. I said yes and asked her about the audience. She said that my audience would mostly be K-12 teachers and administrators. She said that they did get a sprinkling of business people too but I shouldn't worry about that. I honed and updated my previous presentation.

About a week before the conference date, I talked with my colleague once more. Again, I asked about the audience. This time she said that many more business people had registered than usual. After we hung up, I thought about what she had said. What should I do? What would you do? I opened the presentation, saved a copy, opened the copy, and reworked it with more of an eye towards a business audience. One of our university pilots flew me over to the conference. The airport was socked in with fog. It took a bit longer to land than usual and I arrived at the university within minutes of my presentation (against everything I will tell you to do). Again, I asked who my audience would be. I was told "*mostly business people!*" Luckily, I was ready for them! Bring them on! The presentation went smoothly and was well received.

No, no, no! (Not knowing your audience): Several years after the above presentation a group from that same national professional technology organization was invited to present in Shenzhen, China. One of our Chinese members had seen me present and wanted me to do the same presentation in China. I was a well-seasoned presenter by that time with several hundred presentations under my belt. I did my usual. I asked a lot of questions about the audience and I tailored my presentation to what I was told. Towards the end of our China trip we finally arrived in Shenzhen. I met my translator. He asked me a few questions about the presentation. I had sent him a copy so he could translate it several weeks before.

After talking with some conference sponsors and reading over the program I was—well—stunned. My presentation— the one they told me they wanted—had nothing *at all* to do with the conference. It would have been like giving a presentation on motor oil to The Lucky Ladies Quilting Conference.

I had 24 hours to figure out what to do. Luckily, I did have a presentation that would fit or could be easily changed to fit the conference ready on my computer. As a matter of fact, I thought that it would fit perfectly. I was golden! How do I spell relief? L-U-C-K-Y, I thought. I immediately got a hold of my translator and gave him a copy of the new presentation so he could look it over and be ready for me. He looked at me in disbelief and absolutely refused to listen to me. He had translated the other presentation and that was what we were going to give… period. Now put yourself in my shoes. You walk into a full room knowing that the presentation is something that does not fit the conference in any—ANY—way, shape, or form. You sit on the stage knowing that the audience will have absolutely no interest in what you are going to say. Probably two thirds of the audience walked out well before the end. I would have done the same thing. It was a dismal failure. Unfortunately, many of the presenters I have spoken with take their audience for granted. Even if you 'just' present to second-year nursing students, that mindset is not something that you should have.

Several years ago I was in Provincetown, Massachusetts during 'Women's Week'. One of the town historians was conducting a walking tour of places where notable female artists, writers, and actors had lived, worked, and played. I knew little of P-town at the time, so I decided to go on the tour. I left about two-thirds of the way through! It was nothing as stated. The guide just walked around and gave what was probably his usual canned 'tourist' presentation. I can't even remember if he ever mentioned the word 'woman'. He seemed to be enjoying himself though, and I don't think that he ever realized what people thought.

Knowing your audience and their expectations is crucial to your presentation. You should analyze your audience before you ever start to develop (or rework) your presentation. From my stories, I think you should understand that audience analysis does not stop until you have walked *out* of the room at the end of your presentation. Don't take anything for granted. *Anything!* How can you make a presentation really relevant to your audience if you don't have exceptional knowledge of who they are?

Here are a few pieces of information that you should try to find out about your audience before you even accept an invitation to speak:

- Who will be attending my presentation? (users, trainers, students, administrators)
- What are their demographics? (sex, age, religion, ethnicity)
- What business are they in? (finance, education, manufacturing, medical)
- What field(s) are they in?
- How far up the 'chain of command' are they?
- What do they know about the subject? (level of expertise, knowledge base)
- Why will they be attending your presentation? (interest, information, told to attend)
- Will they know the jargon? Acronyms? (Remember: it is always best to have a short aside explanation each time you introduce jargons or acronyms.)
- What do they expect from you?
- What is in it for them? (You really want them to see multiple benefits for the presentation.)
- What argument or evidence will you present? (Will they understand/relate to it?)

See *PoweredGuide 1: Audience Analysis* in Appendix 2 for a handy guide to help you analyze your audience.

Just as an aside: Many how-to presentation guides, books and websites say, 'Be yourself'. By now, you should understand why these authors are not thinking things through. We all say that you can't have a successful presentation if you don't connect with the audience. You can't connect with the audience if you do not know who they are, what their needs

are, and how to get your message across to them. It is more
difficult to connect if you are perceived as an outsider. So...to
present successfully you can't 'be yourself'. You have to be
able to be one of them. This is why you must analyze your
audience and be an actor on a stage!

PoweredPointer 16: Know the room

This is also a good time to start your research into when
you will be presenting, what devices and technical assistance
will be available, and what human help will be available. Of
course this is not always possible at this early stage, but it
beats walking into a room cold. The person asking you to
present may know something about the venue, so don't be
afraid to ask. You should understand any physical attributes
or limitations well before you enter the presentation room.
You really need to know as much information about the
venue as possible even before you start working on your
presentation. You are like the captain on a ship when you are
presenting. You are in charge of everything. Don't leave
anything to chance or to anyone else! See *PoweredGuide 2:
Know the Room* in Appendix 2 for a handy guide to help you
analyze the presentation room.

PoweredPointer 17: Customize, customize, customize!

Never take any audience or any room for granted! All
audiences are different. This could be your fourth presentation to a bakers' union audience. Members of the bakers'
union have certain similarities (they are probably rolling in
dough, for example), but each audience probably has some
different kneads (breads, pastries, pie crusts...) and you must
address your presentation to their kneads. Knowing your
audience is an ongoing task: ongoing from when they enter
the room and ongoing through the end of your presentation
until they exit your presentation. Yes, your audience analysis

continues when they come into your room. You should be ready to meet your audience before they have even stepped into the room. Meeting them is not always possible. Perhaps the presenter before you decided that he would rather answer questions and talk with his audience members, rather than clear away his material so you can set up yours.

Once you are set up, you should try to move around the room, introduce yourself, and chat with several audience members. This will help you better understand who your audience members are. See *PoweredGuide 7: Meeting Your Audience* in Appendix 2 at the end of the book for a handy guide to help you talk to your audience before your presentation.

There are other very good reasons for talking with audience members beforehand. One very important reason is that it will actually help to reduce your anxiety both before and during the presentation. More on this later. Again: You should be reading your audience throughout your presentation and stop only after the last person leaves the room. Watch your audience closely throughout your presentation. Are you getting positive or negative feedback from the audience? Is there a smile or frown, a positive or negative nod or facial expression anywhere? Are they talking with their neighbor or playing on their cell phone? If you are getting any negative feedback, you should try to tweak your presentation on the fly. Perhaps you just have to stop to explain some point in more detail. Later, when I talk about preparation, I will again stress NOT to memorize your presentation word for word. There are several reasons why I say this. For now, let's just emphasize that since you don't have your presentation in memory word for word, you should be able to adjust it as needed to more closely match your audience. Remember, your job, like an actor on the stage, is to get your information across as easily and efficiently as possible. To do this effectively you need a receptive audience. To have a receptive audience you have to understand who they are and what their wants and needs are.

PoweredPointer 18: Give them a reason to pay attention

At this point, you should also have a very good idea about the makeup of your audience. There are at least two reasons for people to be in attendance. The first group is the people who have to be there. They could have been told to be there or perhaps are required to be there for CEUs (Continuing Education Units are sometimes required to keep a job or a license). A second group is composed of those individuals who really want to be there. I guess that there is a third group. This would be the casual observer. Some of these people may have a passing interest; others may just be looking for a place to sit down during a busy conference!

Knowing your audience is really important. Many novice presenters fail to adequately analyze their audience. You may want to find out about them even before you accept the presentation invitation. If you have not done so, take few minutes to look at *PoweredGuide 1: Audience Analysis* in Appendix 2 at the end of the book.

CHAPTER 5

DESIGNING YOUR PRESENTATION

Many people feel that designing a presentation is almost as difficult as standing in front of the audience. I never found this to be the case, as long as I had enough time to adequately prepare before the presentation that is. Message here: DON'T leave anything to the last minute! You know (a) the message, and (b) the audience. Now you just have to put (a) into your presentation medium in a way that (b) will understand and be receptive to it. Your medium will most likely be PowerPoint, although it could also be a whiteboard, flip chart, or just your voice and gestures. In the next chapter we will discuss some important PowerPoint design elements.

It is important that you know why you are giving the presentation. Is it for a commendation or the giving/receiving of an award? Or is it to teach or inform, stimulate, call to action, provoke, or stir up the audience? And while we are at it, will the presentation be serious or can it be more light-hearted and fun?

Your presentation will have three parts: an introduction, a body, and a conclusion. Put another way, first you will get your audience interested and hook them (introduction), then you'll build up your information (body), and last you'll tie everything up with a nice, neat bow (conclusion). It is best for you to remember these three parts as you put your presentation together.

The key to an easily understood presentation is to have your content set in a concrete and sequential order. OK, so some of you are random thinkers. Even you will find that it is not very difficult to put your ideas down in a concrete, sequential order. You have to!

PoweredPointer 19: Your presentation should be concrete and sequential

There are many popular definitions for the terms 'goal' and 'objective'. These words each have a very specific meaning. The verb used in either the goal or objective statement is the key. Think 'what is the verb?' when you try to figure out whether a statement is a goal or an objective. A goal is a general statement of what you are trying to accomplish. That is all. Just a *general statement.* Remember the verb. Goals are not written using a verb that you can measure. I will repeat that. The verb in a goal is *not* measurable. What do we mean by the verb is not measurable?

The easiest way to think about it is that the verb you see in your goal statement cannot be used as a verb in a test question. If you can't use the verb in a test question, you can't measure the action the verb is describing. In this case, the verb in your goal statement is not a measurable verb. Therefore it is a good verb to use in a goal statement. Examples of verbs that can't be measured include learn, appreciate, understand, and know. These verbs won't work in a test question. For example: Goal Statement: *Appreciate the plays of Shakespeare* does not work as a test question: "OK students, here is the test. It is only one question: *Appreciate* the plays of Shakespeare. How would you measure "appreciate"? Your ultimate goal may be to get your students to appreciate the plays of Shakespeare. But you cannot use or measure the verb 'appreciate'.

If the verb can't be measured, it may be a good verb to

use in your goal statement. A goal should be a simple sentence. It should be the reason you are giving your presentation. Is the presentation informative? Is it persuasive? A well-written goal might be, for example: *The (audience) will learn (verb) about sexual harassment in the workplace.* Remember I just said that the verb in a goal can't be used in a test question. The verb *'Learn'* does not work as a test question: *Learn* (same verb as in goal) *about sexual harassment in the workplace.* If this were the test question, how would the student answer it? Do you understand what I am getting at?

Objectives, on the other hand, are very precise. They are very specific and use measurable (action) verbs. A verb in an objective is the same verb that you will use in your test question. Examples of measurable verbs are: describe, list, solve, demonstrate, compare, and assemble. To carry this discussion through to its final conclusion, objectives also contain the criterion used for the evaluation. Objectives indicate what the person will be doing when he is being tested on the objective. *The student will list five examples of sexual harassment in the workplace.* Again, you will notice that a good objective verb will be a good test question. The verb in this objective is 'list': *List* (same verb as in objective) *five* (criterion) *examples of sexual harassment in the workplace.* Objectives state exactly what you want in the answer the student gives in order to answer the test question. Objectives do not include how you will evaluate their answer though. This is not a good objective: *List four out of five examples of sexual harassment in the workplace.* Four out of five is how you will *evaluate* the objective. In this case you want to cover five examples in your discussion but are happy if they remember only four of the examples. It is not what you are planning to teach them. 'Goal', 'objective', and 'evaluation' are interrelated but have very different and separate meanings. (In this example, if you are happy that the audience will walk out knowing only four out of five examples, why not just teach the audience four examples? You will reduce your workload by 20%.)

The father of modern corporate management is a man

named Peter Drucker. In his 1954 book *The Practice of Management* Drucker described S.M.A.R.T. objectives. S.M.A.R.T. is an acronym for Specific, Measurable, Achievable, Realistic, and Time-bound (Drucker, 1954). Well done, Mr. Drucker!

Time for a quick review

- **Goal:** The (audience) will learn (the immeasurable verb) about sexual harassment in the workplace.
- **Objective:** The (audience member) will list (the measurable verb) five (the criterion) examples of sexual harassment in the workplace.
- **Test question:** List five examples of sexual harassment in the workplace.
- **Evaluation:** It is up to you. For example, they could list all five examples for credit, with each of the listed examples worth one point.

- **Goal:** Students will learn how to construct a model of a teepee used by Lipan Apache Indians.
- **Objective:** Given six plastic soda straws, one foot of string, one 16" by 24" sheet of construction paper, and cellophane tape and scissors, the student will construct a model of a Lipan Apache teepee. This model will include a properly sized and scaled pole and covering arrangement, entranceway, smoke outlet, and pole top arrangement.
- **Test question:** Given six plastic soda straws, one foot of string, one 16" by 24" sheet of construction paper, and scissors and cellophane tape, construct (measurable verb) a model of a Lipan Apache Indian teepee. The model must include a properly sized and scaled (criteria) pole

and skin arrangement, entranceway, smoke outlet, and pole top arrangement.

- **Evaluation:** This depends on how much weight you want to give to each of the eight parts listed above.

Write down your presentation goal and follow that with one to three objectives. You are not interested in test questions or evaluations at this time. But you should have some ideas of what your audience should know in mind, although I am sure you won't give the audience a test at the end of your presentation! Remember to use simple sentences. The number of objectives depends on the length of the presentation. A general rule of thumb is to have one objective per 30 minutes of presentation time (ACHA, 2019). The objectives are the supporting points that build towards your goal.

Now write down any arguments or supporting details for each of your objectives. Don't worry about writing down an introduction or conclusion at this time. When you have written down your arguments, read over what you have written to make sure they follow in a proper developmental order. Each objective you listed should build on the previous one. A good presentation is like building a brick wall. Each objective is like a layer. You start your presentation at ground level and add the next objectives layer by layer until the wall is finished. Your finished brick completes your goal. See *Powered-Guide 3: Planning Your Presentation* in Appendix 2 for a handy guide to help you plan your presentation.

Goal:
Objective One:
Argument or details
Argument or details
Argument or details
Etc.
Objective Two:
Argument or details
Etc.

PoweredPointer 20: Write down your goal and one to three objectives

Are you satisfied with what you are going to say? Does the order of your presentation make sense? Does each step build on the previous one? Later, as you review your notes and recording of your presentation and review feedback from those who have volunteered to listen to one of your run-throughs, you will probably need and/or want to adjust parts of it. We all find things we want or need to change. It is called polishing your presentation, and it does not stop until you finish reviewing your audience comments after the presentation is over.

Time to write your introduction

Once you are very clear on your goals and objectives, it is time to write an introduction. Your introduction should be clear and it should introduce the major points you wish to cover in your following monologue. It should also set the tone for your presentation. This could be just a short discussion associated with your 'What we will cover' slide (which is usually your second slide at the beginning of your presentation). I don't like to stand up in front of people while someone is introducing me, so I introduce myself. (Remember I did not want a retirement party!) Most room monitors are very happy to let you do this. My first slide, like yours, contains the title of the presentation and my name and title/affiliation. After this you should put in an attention grabber. Give them a reason why it is important for them to stay until the conclusion of your presentation. How will your presentation be useful to your audience? What problem/s will it help them solve? Why should your audience bother sitting through your presentation? If you can't think of a good reason for them to stay for your entire presentation, well…you and your audience might as well all go and have a cup of coffee instead. Follow this with some background on the topic and a bit about what you hope to accomplish.

Here are some helpful ways to introduce your presentation:

Ask a question

The question should be something that links your presentation to your audience. This is a great way to involve your audience and get them to internalize your topic. A good question gives them a sense of belonging and control; some may even say 'power'. What do you think a school (librarian/media specialist's) number-one fear is as they go about their day? What are some important things to do before you actually start to put together your presentation? Why do you think the folks in human resources made this presentation compulsory?

Cite a startling statistic

This can be a great way to really get the audience involved with your topic. It can frame your topic with an irrefutable frame of reference. A startling statistic makes the rest of your topic more credible. For example:

 "53% of Americans visited the library in 2012. Three years later (2015) that number dropped to 44%—no, that is not a 9% drop but a 12%

drop. What do you think visitation percentages are now?"

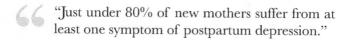 "Just under 80% of new mothers suffer from at least one symptom of postpartum depression."

"The odds of being killed by a shark in US waters are one in 250 million. The odds of being killed by a vending machine are one in 112 million. A vending machine is twice as dangerous as a shark. Oh yes, the odds of being killed by a cow are one in 12.5 million. Cows are 20 times more dangerous than sharks...and ten times more dangerous than vending machines."

"The odds of drowning at the beach are one in 18 million. Fourteen times more probable than being killed by a shark."

"Every year between 100,000 and 200,000 people die in hospitals because of medical mistakes."

Just make sure that your statistic is relevant to your presentation.

Make a dramatic announcement or statement

For example:

"Warren Buffett, one of the most successful business men in the world, was so terrified of public speaking that when he was in college he would do whatever he could to choose classes where he did not have to get up in front of people."

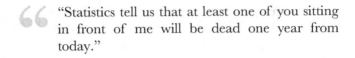

"Statistics tell us that at least one of you sitting in front of me will be dead one year from today."

"You have germs in your mouth from everyone you ever kissed and anyone they ever kissed before they kissed you."

"On a good day, a woodchuck could chuck about 700 pounds of wood. If a woodchuck could chuck wood."

Again, just make sure it is relevant!

Read a quote from a book, newspaper, or magazine

It would be best to quote an expert who agrees with you. This adds credibility to your message. Using a quote that does not agree with you can also be helpful. You just have to explain how it is relevant and why it empowers your argument.

Relate a personal experience

I have done that many times in this book.

Tell a story that has a twist at the end

For example:

"In 1994 J.K. Rowling was divorced, on government aid, and could barely afford to feed her child. She was so poor that she used an old typewriter to make copies of her first 90,000-word *Harry Potter* book. After a dozen rejections, the very small London publisher *Bloomsbury* decided to publish it because the editor's eight-year-old daughter was crazy about it. The publisher agreed to publish it for his daughter but also told Rowling to get a day job since she wouldn't make much money writing children's books. In May of 2019, *The Sunday Times* of London estimated J.K. Rowling's net worth at just under a billion dollars."

Use an 'imagine' scenario

Of course it has to be relevant to the topic. For example:

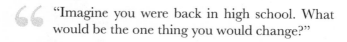

"Imagine you were back in high school. What would be the one thing you would change?"

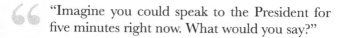

"Imagine you could speak to the President for five minutes right now. What would you say?"

Say something funny

This can be very powerful, but it can also be a big mistake. Good jokes can loosen up your audience and make them— and you—feel more at ease. Bad jokes can be a disaster. I once started a very lighthearted keynote speech by walking in with a newspaper and a very straight face. I apologized for bringing up what I was about to say but I felt that it is very relevant to the discussion. I lifted the paper with a sad face and said "It seems that Larry LaPrise, the man who wrote the Hokey Pokey, died last week at the age of 83." (*Short pause with sad face.*) "It says that he died peacefully." (*Pause and deep sigh.*) "Something really sad and unfortunate happened though." (*Another pause and deep sigh.*) "It seems that in the funeral home they had a lot of trouble placing him in his casket." (*Pause, sad expression, sigh.*) "It seems they put his right foot in," (*Short pause.*) "they took his right foot out," (*Shorter pause.*) "they put his right foot back in and," (*Short pause.*) "shook it all…" That set the tone for what followed.

Use a 'what if' scenario

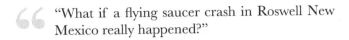 "What if a flying saucer crash in Roswell New Mexico really happened?"

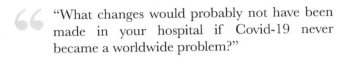 "What changes would probably not have been made in your hospital if Covid-19 never became a worldwide problem?"

Summarize several main points you will cover

Remember, your introduction is as important as your presentation itself. It is even possible that it could make or totally break it. It is so important to start off on the right foot, so to speak. Take your time with it and ask the people previewing your presentation what they think about it.

PoweredPointer 21: Jumpstart your presentation with a real attention grabber

And last but not least: your conclusion!

It is now time to write your conclusion. Your conclusion should summarize your objectives and bring your presentation to a logical end. Refer to your introduction in your conclusion if possible. Return to your attention grabber. Put in a call to action. End on a high note!

Here are some ways to end your presentation. You will recognize many of them as ways to introduce your presentation.

- *Link it back to the beginning.* Did you tell a story in the beginning? Did you ask a question? Look back at what you did in your introduction and say it, do it, or link it to your conclusion.
- *Play a short video or audio clip* that will really hit home

and emphasize your point. Just make sure it is highly relevant to your goal and audience.

- *Come up with a quirky slogan.* Keep it short and memorable. Make sure the slogan summarizes your presentation. Oftentimes, looking back at your goal helps you formulate a slogan. There is something called "The rule of threes". Quite simply, it states that beliefs, ideas, and concepts (geez, that is also a 'three') are more interesting and memorable if presented in threes. "I came, I saw, I conquered!"—"Veni, Vidi, Vici," (Julius Caesar). "Get Brexit done"! (British Prime Minister Boris Johnson). "There are three kinds of lies: lies, damned lies, and statistics"! (Benjamin Disraeli). "Location, location, location!" (The woman who sold me my house.)

- *Ask a provocative or rhetorical question.* Something that will stay with the audience and make them think. "What will happen if we don't do such and such??"

- *Introduce a clock.* "Time is short, get to work!"

- *Show a relevant cartoon.* There are plenty of them out there, but of course, whether you can or should use one depends on the reason and tone of your presentation. If you do use a cartoon, credit the source: "Here is something I found on the Birdman Website that seems to sum things up!"

- *Give your audience that last surprising fact.* You may want to keep one last surprising fact as a sendoff.

- *Call the audience to action.* Inspire your audience to attack a problem. What would happen if they don't act or how will circumstances change if they do?

- *Give them a choice.* If you do this, what will happen? What will happen if you do not follow through?

- *Summarize what you have said.* This is the most

common conclusion, but you can do better with a
little thought.

- *Tell a story.* Something emotional and thought provoking that tugs at the heartstrings but still ties everything together.
- *Relate a personal experience.* Something that will tie everything together. As you have read, I have used personal experiences throughout the book. I have also used them with good results in presentation conclusions.
- *Read to them.* A powerful quote from a book, newspaper, or magazine.

PoweredPointer 22: Your conclusion should be just the beginning for your audience

You should now have the critical parts down on paper.

It is time to fill out your presentation

Wow, you have finished your presentation! Or have you?

Start at the beginning and go over everything you have written down. Yes, I know you have just written down a bare skeleton of what you are going to present. But is it in a logical order? Does it make sense? Does it flow? This is really important. Presentations start at a specific point and build up to the conclusion. Does your outline do this? This building process might not be easy. If you were going to give a talk on the six New England states, for example, what would be your 'big' conclusion? How do you build up a list of six New England states? There are six New England States? Your presentation still has to have flow. You need a thread that ties everything together. In this example, is it industry, tourism, history, entrance to the union, or something else? Of course, much of this depends on the reason you are giving the talk in the first place. Are you satisfied with the order of your thoughts? If so, go back to your outline and fill in the details. This could include more details on each point, supporting data, history, examples, etc. You might even include some fun facts or quotations. Again, what you put in at this point really depends on who your audience will be.

The next very important point I want to get across to you is this: You should think of your presentation as a peanut. What do I mean by this?

Buy a bag of unshelled peanuts. Not the ones that are soaked in salt, though. Too much salt is not good for your health. (Don't buy peanuts if you are allergic to them. If you are, please forget that I asked you to purchase peanuts.) Free five peanuts from the bag. (See how words are important? If I had said "*Take* five peanuts from the bag" instead that sentence might have a very different connotation! (Connotation: what a word implies or suggests. Even though they both denote [*literal meaning*] the same thing!) Open each peanut. Now, take any one of these peanuts and eat it. (Again, if you are allergic, forget I said that.) With any luck, the peanut you are eating tastes almost like any of the other peanuts you have eaten in your life. Eat another one and see if you would say that the second peanut has a peanut taste. You now know the taste 'essence' of what we call a 'peanut'. In the case of a peanut the 'essence', what make a peanut a peanut is how it looks, tastes, smells, etc. It is how it differs from all other legumes. Each peanut you take out of the shell will probably taste a little different, but they each will have enough peanut qualities in order for someone who has never seen or eaten a peanut to identify them as a peanut after they have eaten a few. If you were new to the peanut world and you only saw or ate one of them, you would most likely be able to identify another sample as a 'peanut'. I know, sometimes you open a peanut and get a real ringer. It could be burnt and/or shriveled up. Notice though that each peanut you open up is also a little different. If you had chosen a different peanut to start with you would still 'know' what a peanut is: its 'essence'.

Notice that I started by saying "Buy a bag of unshelled

peanuts", and "If you only saw one of them." Visuals are very important. (More on this later.)

PoweredPointer 23: Think of your presentation as a peanut

The 'essence' of your presentation, what distinguishes it from other presentations is the information you have put into your presentation and how you placed it in there. The way you put it in: the order, the building of ideas, makes your presentation different from other presentations. The 'essence' of your presentation is carried to the audience through your PowerPoint bullet points. (Some people call bullets 'reveals' since they reveal information.) Remember, as long as you examine or eat one peanut you should have the general idea of the essence or flavor of most other peanuts. As long as you present each bullet of information, your audience will understand the essence of each point you are making in your presentation. You should use each bullet point in your Power-Point as a starting point to explain that point in more detail. Remember though, your bullet points are the essence of your presentation. Just as all peanuts are different, any presentation you build around your PowerPoint bullets will be different. How can that be?? You may not/do not have to say the same thing each time you explain, for example, the third bullet on your fifth slide. The PowerPoint bullets contain the information you want to get across. Anything else you add smooths out your presentation, helps your audience remember, and adds additional information to help the bulleted information sink in. Your presentation is the whole peanut. Your bullet points are the essence of your presentation.

For those of you with a peanut allergy: This morning I was working at a non-profit theater. Along with a sandwich at lunch I was given a bag of Cape Cod potato chips. On the back of the bag this was written: "No two chips are identical but they all share a hearty potato flavor and that wonderful Cape Cod crunch." The *essence* of a Cape Cod potato chip...

PoweredPointer 24: Your bullets are your presentation

Your bullets are your presentation. In a way, you can even say that you are speaking extemporaneously around each bullet—*although with a heck of a lot of practice*—speaking from an outline—*your bullet points*—of key words and phrases!

When you actually stand in front of your audience and present, you will not have memorized all your content. If you have to present a speech without the use of PowerPoint, you could just do it from note cards using the same steps you used to develop a PowerPoint presentation. If you are lucky enough to have a PowerPoint presentation, you will use the bullet points in your PowerPoint as a springboard for your thoughts. You will ad-lib the rest of it from your memory. After all, you will have rehearsed what you would like to cover many times. Your presentation will not be the same every time, but remember that the points you are trying (needing) to get across are all presented as bullets on your visuals or listed on your note cards.

As you develop your presentation, you may want to jot down a few notes for each bullet to help cue your memory as to what information to cover on each visual. Review these notes every time you rehearse your presentation. If you do this, you should be able to include what you want to include and not need supplemental notes in front of you as you present in front of the audience.

Let's review, in order, the first steps you have to perform to put together your presentation:

- State your main idea (goal).
- List your objectives.
- Outline the points to cover (arguments) to support each objective.
- Write your introduction.
- Write your conclusion.

When you reach this point, you will have a good idea of who you are going to present to. You will have your goal and objectives, supporting information for each objective, and your introduction and conclusion.

Now we have to go over exactly how to put your information into a PowerPoint presentation!

CHAPTER 6

PRESENTATION GRAPHICS: WHAT MICROSOFT POWERPOINT DESIGNERS DO NOT UNDERSTAND AND HOW TO FIX THAT

E verything you write down in your presentation outline is subject to change. As you actually put together your presentation, work with it, and repeatedly go over it, you will tinker with the content, add or remove points and information, and perhaps even change the order for a smoother flow. If your presentation is a speech or a keynote, you may even decide that you want to go back and start from square one. All of this is normal. If you have to give your presentation, speech or keynote again at a later date, don't be surprised if you change parts of it each time you give it, even if it was very well received when you last presented it. You should always be trying to make your presentation, speech, or keynote better. Besides, if you find yourself in the position to give your presentation, speech, or keynote again, you will have to do another audience and location analysis in order to tailor your content for the new group and location. You may want to update factual information or sharpen your material to fit the new audience better.

Time to get physical

Before you start to put your presentation together, we should discuss its actual physical construction. In this chapter I am going to talk about what you need to know and how you should construct your PowerPoint slides. In a pinch you could use a flip chart (prepared in advance) or perhaps even a whiteboard or chalkboard (so 20th century! Yikes!) The criteria I am about to discuss can be applied to a PowerPoint presentation, posters, blackboards, whiteboards, or even paper mounted on an easel.

Using visuals in your presentation

Your presentation slides are a vital part of your presentation. The text and visuals on your slides will determine how your points come across and the extent to which the audience will retain the information. Your slide content will also help set the pacing of the presentation. In short, your slides will make or break your presentation. This is why it's so important to have high quality, succinct, and accurate presentation slides. Below are some examples of common mistakes people make with their slides:

- *Poor-quality visuals.* (We will discuss how to design good visuals later!)
- *Irrelevant content.* Sometimes we have little tidbits of information, an aside, or a comment we would like to include. Please be very careful with this. You do not want to do anything that will break the audiences' train of thought. If it is really important, add it as a bullet, otherwise it is probably best to drop it.
- *Outdated content.* Come on now. It takes three seconds (OK, maybe 30 seconds) to change the information on a PowerPoint slide. You won't look professional if you have to say that the information on this or that slide is wrong or outdated. If you do, your audience might feel offended. Indeed, they *should* feel offended since you did not bother

taking even 30 seconds to replace the incorrect information!

- *Content that does not suit your audience.* Make sure that your visuals and bullet points are designed specifically for your audience. If you are using the same presentation for several audiences, you may only have to change one or a few things to customize it. There are ways to customize your presentation by using only the information you want.

- *Content to fill time or hide behind.* If you ran through several rehearsals of your presentation, as you should have, you will have a good idea of how long it will take. No fillers, please. You can (should) always make room for questions at the end. This is a better way to fill in extra time. (I will discuss a surefire way to win at question time later.) Research does show that a typical presentation takes less time when you are standing in front of the audience, so you should have some 'fillers' in the wings just in case.

When would we use a visual? That is easy. In order to:

- *Clarify a point.* Seeing something in writing or supported by a picture or illustration can help your audience get a better grasp on the concept you are trying to get across.

- *Emphasize a point.* If you put your information in a visual and bring attention to it, most people will think it must be important and hopefully attend to it.

- *Change focus.* It is easier to change your focus if you move on to a new visual. The new visual will break from the old thought and give you a much smoother transition to the new material.

- *Increase retention.* Research has shown that the more

senses that are involved in any learning situation, the higher the retention rate. If you make a statement, the person hears you and perhaps writes it down. (Hear, process, write: three senses.) If you have the same statement in a visual the person sees the statement, hears the statement (every time you 'unmask' a new part of a visual you should also repeat it), processes it, and writes it down. (See, hear, process, write: four senses.)

- *Add variety.* Visuals break up the monotony of your speech. No offense, but just having you standing up there and talk to us is not very exciting... unless you are really famous, extraordinarily handsome, or drop-dead gorgeous. Later on we will discuss why you don't want to go overboard by constructing overly exciting visuals. We have already discussed how you should look.
- *Keep people on their toes.* Visuals add variety to your presentation. They give the audience something to look at instead of just listening to you talk, looking out the window, or checking their email on their phones. Ask questions even if you don't want answers as you reveal your points. Thankfully, most rooms where you will do your presentation will not have windows.
- *Enhance your image.* Research has shown that audiences feel that people who use visuals are better prepared and are better masters of the subject area.
- *Distract your audience.* Visuals give you time to do things that may not be noticed by most of your audience. This could be your time to take a little drink, slip a mint into your mouth, or adjust an article of clothing.

Ultimately however, there is only one encompassing rule to keep in mind as you construct a presentation slide:

- *Keep it simple.* You don't want your audience to be overwhelmed by the content. They should be able to see a bullet, quickly process it, and move their attention back to you in a matter of seconds. (More on this a little bit later.)

PoweredPointer 25: Keep it simple

Just how simple do I mean? I will give you an example. Let us say that you were giving a talk on consumerism in the United States and came to the subject of consumer complaints. You found a website that listed the top ten complaint categories, how many complaints there were, and the percentage of complaints contained in each category (FTC, 2017). Let's put the top five consumer complaints on a slide.

Consumer Complaints

The Federal Trade Commission published a summary of consumer complaints for 2017. The greatest number of complaints (28%) was 'Debt Collection'. This was followed by 'Imposter Scams' (13%), 'Identity Theft' (12.9%) and 'Telephone and Mobile Services' (10%). Tied for fifth place was 'Banks and Lenders' and 'Prizes, Sweepstakes and Lotteries' each with 5% of the total complaints.

What do you think? Simple? Well, not really. I think you can see that it would take an audience member several minutes to read and process the information on this slide. What do you think about the following revision? Remember that each bullet would be shown and explained one at a time in sequence.

Consumer Complaints

*Debt Collection (28%)

*Imposter Scams (13%)

*Identity Theft (12.9%)

* Telephone and Mobile Services (10%)

*(Tied each with 5%)
  Banks and Lenders
  Prizes, Sweepstakes and Lotteries

You can see that this version is much better. It is much simpler and easier to understand since each bullet would be revealed and explained one at a time. But it should be even simpler:

Consumer Complaints

*Debt Collection

*Imposter Scams

*Identity Theft

* Telephone and Mobile Services

*(Tied)
  Banks and Lenders
  Prizes, Sweepstakes and Lotteries

This last example is the ideal way to present the information on the slide. You can't say that it is not simple. Your audience members must hear, process, and activate their fingers to write down all the other information you will present. They will also look at the information and reprocess it to make sure it was written down correctly. A good way to add audience interaction at this time would be to show the list on a separate slide and give the audience a few minutes to rank the items themselves. Tell them not to write anything down because you will be showing them the proper order and make comments about each complaint after they have had a few minutes to rank the complaints. After a discussion or a vote, you could present a second slide containing just the title and ask the group for number one. Now, just reveal your first bullet and discuss it. Do the same for the rest of the list. By doing this you have added audience participation, and perhaps even some fun, to your presentation.

Most people use one of the several presentation templates that are readily available in a presentation package such as Microsoft PowerPoint. You can also download hundreds of free templates from the Web. Templates are very powerful and make putting together a presentation quick and easy. Perhaps I should say that the templates found in presentation packages allow you to put together a presentation that is quick and easy. Unfortunately, most people simply go right to the templates, choose the one that they like or feel will work best —or the one they always use—and start filling it in. Don't do that.

 "It (PowerPoint) has historically been a tool that promoted stupid things, like creating audience-abuse slides that no one could read and presentations where the presenter read the slide to the audience. People… found it so easy to build presentations they'd wait until the last minute and then get in front of an audience with little or no rehearsal or preparation, resulting in substandard performance." (States noted presenter and Computerworld contributor Rob Enderle, 2020).

Software engineers are great designers of software, but poor designers of presentation templates. I sometimes wonder why those big companies don't have software engineers and visual designers working together, or at least have visual designers who actually have spent a good deal of time 'in the trenches' presenting. Well-designed slides should carry information to the viewer. Presentation slides should not 'WOW' or distract the viewer or take on a life of their own. Most of the templates in software packages use 'WOW' or at least 'wow' that many times might distract the viewer. Let's take a look at some features you should incorporate to make your slides help you get your points across while not distracting from your audiences' learning experience.

Guidelines for lettering

Always use a sans-serif typeface such as Helvetica or Arial. Typefaces can be divided into two large groups: serif typefaces and sans-serif typefaces. Serif typefaces have little decorative parts at the ends of each letter stroke. Think of a capitol 'T' in a newspaper headline. The top horizontal line of the 'T' had a small projection hanging off at each end. There are also small projections (called feet) on each side at the bottom of the vertical line. These projections are called serifs. Most books and newspapers are written using a serif typeface. Sans means no or not, so a sans-serif typeface is a typeface without serifs. Research has shown that sans-serif (without serifs) typefaces are easier to read when the words are projected. Research has also shown that serif typefaces (with the serifs) are easier to read in written form, such as in a book or newspaper.

- *Use upper and lower case letters.* Do not write in all caps. Sentences in which the words are written using both upper and lower case letters are easier to read.
- *Try to use just two type sizes.* Using many type sizes tends to draw attention to the text and away from the information it contains.
- *Each slide should contain a maximum of five or six lines or*

bullets made up of no more than five or six words in each line. This is a good general rule of thumb. If you try to follow this rule you will not have too many lines or words on each slide, the words will not be crammed onto the visual, and the words will be large enough for everyone to easily see. Each bullet should take no more than one or two seconds for an audience member to read *and to process.*

- *Shadow your font.* That little bit of shadowing around the letters helps them stand out from the background just a bit more.

- *Use a horizontal (landscape) format.* I mention this because I have actually seen several presentations that were in a vertical (portrait) format. We like to read long lines of type, not a few words, next line, a few words, next line, etc. Of course, your medium may change this. For example, if you were using flip charts this would be difficult to do.

Top Five (+) Points to Remember

*Sans-serif font (Helvetica/Arial)

*Upper and lower case

*Just two type sizes

* Five to six lines and words

*Shadow your font

General slide guidelines

- *Use a consistent slide format.* As I stated, text and visuals should not detract from your presentation.

They should not be the 'star'. Your slides are the medium (like you), not the message. It is very easy to change background colors, text colors, add multiple typefaces and all sorts of animations and sounds with the click of a mouse. Don't!

- *Trippple check spelling, grammar, etc.* Things happen. Don't let them. Check and recheck each of your slides. It would be a good idea to get a trusted friend to go over them. You may be surprised at what they come up with! It is interesting and probably sad in a way: I use this misspelling (trippple) in the visual I use when I talk about presentation graphics. Less than half of the time someone will point out that the word is misspelled. Sometimes I even pause a bit longer after I show that bullet to see if I get any response! Perhaps they are just being nice. Reading a piece back to front can be really helpful for spotting errors. It takes the mind out of effortless understanding mode and helps it spot errors it would normally gloss over.
- *Non-projected letters should be at least one inch tall per 15 feet of visual distance from the furthest audience member.* Projected letters should be at least 48 points for headers and 36 points for each bullet that follows. Make sure that the letters on the screen are still meeting the minimum of one inch per 15 feet of distance.
- *Don't use sounds in your bullets.* Sounds are distracting. Presentation applications give you the ability to add rocket sounds, sloshes, gunshots, dogs barking, and many, many other sounds. Don't!
- *Use numbers and bullets correctly.*
- *Numbers send a message.* Use numbers to show order of importance or chronological order. Including numbers will actually slow down processing of the bullet since the numbers are subconsciously

perceived as being part of the message and hence increases processing time.

- *Unnumbered bullets are generic:* Unnumbered bullets indicate equal importance and more importantly, they don't distract from the words. Notice that I have not numbered any of the items in this list of lettering guidelines. (They are all of equal importance!) Interestingly though, sometimes unnumbered lists are called 'ordered lists'!

- *Reveal your bullets one at a time, and only when you have finished the bullet point you are on and are ready to discuss the next point.* Otherwise your audience members will be busy copying down the whole slide and conceivably not hear or process your comments on the bullet you are still explaining. (We all do that!) This is important. Give your audience time to write down the bullet. You may want to say the bullet out loud as you reveal it. I usually do. It helps audience members process the bullet, gives them time to write it down, and also gives you a few seconds to collect your thoughts. If you are writing the bullet on a flip chart or white/blackboard, say it out loud as you write it down. After you have finished writing, step aside so the audience can see the bullet and write it down if they've not done so already.

Guidelines for quotations

Quotations are not a part of your presentation. You are taking something from outside your presentation and putting it into your presentation. Quotations are usually not your own words but someone else's. Perhaps I could say that it is a "foreign intruder" into your presentation. Because of this you have to set the words apart in a particular way. You should keep quotations short, place the words in an inverted pyramid shape, italicize the lettering, and use a serif typeface. Please make sure you credit the source!

> *"If you must use quotations: few words,*
> *inverted pyramid, italicize, and*
> *use serif typeface."*

PoweredPointer 26: Incorporate the lettering, color, and quotation design points

Guidelines for charts and graphs

- *Don't copy and paste charts or graphs into your presentation.* You should redesign the chart or graph specifically for your presentation. Reproduce only the data you need and remember the visual distance guidelines.
- *Make it big.* Don't scrunch your chart or graph into just one part of your visual. Instead, take up as much space as you can. In most cases, the bigger the better. This includes not only the actual chart but also its annotations and labels.
- *Use large fonts for annotations and labels.* They should be easy to read by anyone in the audience. Often annotations and labels on charts and graphs are much smaller and hence unreadable by many in the audience.
- *Use bright and contrasting colors.* It should be easy to differentiate between chart and graph data on your visual. Shades of a color or gray, pale colors, patterns, or pastel colors should not be used unless there is a specific reason for it, for example when demonstrating a gradual change over time.
- *Don't use multiple colors* - unless you are differentiating data, for example deficit/surplus,

car brands, different clinical techniques, different countries, etc.

- *Avoid 3D effects in bar charts.* You don't want the viewers to wonder or even think about where the top or end of the bar is compared to the axis grid. As with all your visuals: keep it simple!
- *Label your axes.* Make sure that the labels are large, clear, and meaningful. Be specific so your audience will not have to think about what you are trying to show and what your labels mean. Be very careful in your use of abbreviations or acronyms. You don't want to lose audience members here. This also applies to the units you use. Make sure they are easy to understand. It is a good idea to go over and explain your axes labels to make sure that everyone is on the same page.
- *Start your Y-axis with zero.* Research shows that doing otherwise may lead to inaccurate conclusions.
- *Remove 'label clutter'.* Try to use as few words or phrases as possible.
- *Filter the data to focus the information on the chart or graph to highlight just the information you are trying to get across to the audience.*
- *Round off decimal numbers in your labels.* 7.59 should be 7.6, 13.34 should be 13.4, etc. You can even simplify these numbers to 8 and 13 if it still conserves the meaning and idea you are trying to get across.
- *Credit your source!* Give credit where credit is due. And besides, sometimes in the heat of the moment you may forget who said or wrote your quotation!

Guidelines for images

- *Don't use poor quality images.* If you use a small image and you enlarge it on a slide, it may get pixelated or blurry. This will distract from your presentation more than you can imagine. It is better to leave out the image rather than use one of poor quality.

- *Tiny images are out.* Little images placed alone or in groups on a slide are difficult to see and annoying. Avoid this extra fluff. If the image is important, make sure it is big enough to see and understand.
- *WATCH OUT FOR COPYRIGHT.* Google is wonderful but don't consider it an image repository. Have you ever put up a website or a picture on the Web? It could end up on Google images. Most (think to yourself 'all') of these images are owned by someone else. Don't use them unless you can get permission. I received permission from *Weekly World News* to use the 'Hillary Alien' cover I used earlier in the book. I can use it for free until book sales reach a certain level; after that, I will have to pay. There are many royalty-free image sites. Just make sure you abide by the website's specific rules. If you can't find a good royalty-free image, there are also many low-cost image sites online.

Guidelines for color

- *Keep your colors to a minimum.* Use a common background on all your slides. Remember, slide design should not distract your audience. The slide title should be a second color and the bullets should be a third color. I usually use a blue background, yellow title, and white bullets.
- *Choose colors that contrast sharply.* The easier your slides are to read, the faster they are processed and the better they will be at getting your message across.
- *Use light words and a dark background.* Light words on

a dark background are easier to read. Conversely, dark words on a light background are harder to read. The words also appear to be smaller. Remember, large people sometimes wear dark clothing to look slimmer and fade into the background. (Since I usually present in a dark suit or sports coat, at this time in my presentation I usually stop and tell the audience to "Look at me, (*pause*) I am really morbidly obese but because I am wearing this dark suit I look thin." (I am 5'8" and weigh 143 pounds.) Of course if there is someone in the audience with a bit more poundage you should skip doing this last part out of kindness.

- *Don't use multicolor or busy backgrounds.* Busy backgrounds have a tendency to distract your audience.

A problem with color

When you design your visuals you should think about the combination of colors you use, especially with respect to the color of the background versus the color of the lettering. A good friend of mine was driving me home one night when we were in college. It was a dark, moonless night. He was driving rather fast as we approached a red traffic light. I asked (sarcastically) if he realized that the light was red. He said that he did not and thanked me. While we were stopped at the light, he said that he was color blind and figured out when to stop by looking at the position of the lighted lens on a traffic light. He could not make out the position of the light that night since it was so dark. You probably know at least 10 men. The law of averages say that one of them may be color blind. Really, about 8% of men and 0.5% of women worldwide are red-green colorblind. Another one in 30-50,000 are blue-yellow colorblind. I avoid red-green color combinations and always ask when I show my title slide at the beginning of a presentation if anyone has any difficulty seeing the words on the screen.

The most popular colors in order are blue, green, red, black, brown, and purple. Here are some subconscious perceptions an individual may associate with certain colors:

- **Blue:** Research indicates that blue is the most favored color. Others say that it is the second most powerful color following green. Blue is calming, contemplative, and connotes trust, intelligence, and strength. Blue is my favorite background color.
- **Green:** Growth, movement. Green is said to be the most restful color to the human eye. Perhaps this is because it is such a large part of our natural environment! Green may have negative connotations for a small portion of people: green with envy; looking a bit green around the gills.
- **Red:** Red commands attention! It connotes power, boldness, and excitement. It can also connote deficit spending, blood, and danger.
- **Black:** Black connotes elegance, power, authority, and control. It could also connote sophistication. I have taken to wearing a lot of black clothing as I have gotten older.
- **Brown:** Brown is hard to use in a presentation. To many people it just doesn't look right. Brown is a naturally abundant color and connotes natural things. Unfortunately, some of these things could be mud, dirt, and bodily...stuff.
- **Purple:** Purple is associated with integrity, spirituality, creativity, and royalty.
- **Yellow:** Yellow is the first color the human eye notices! Some people see yellow as uplifting and cheerful. It can also connote caution, sickness, and dislike.

Please remember the guidelines I went over in this chapter and try to incorporate them as you prepare your presentation's slides. Remember that the information you put on your slides represents the main information you want to get across —the essence of your presentation. You should go over your presentation enough times so you can confidently use each bullet as a starting point to flesh out what you are presenting. It's really important that your presentation medium doesn't overshadow your message.

PoweredPointer 27: Remember the visual design points

After you have designed and constructed your presentation slides it is time for you to put them aside for three or four days. Don't look at them, and try not to think about your presentation. Get a few days distance from your work. You may be surprised that you may actually see things that you simply glossed over in your mind as you prepared your visuals. After three or four days, take out your outline and look it over. Read over your introduction. If you were an audience member, would you stay around to hear the presentation? Now look at the conclusion. Is your conclusion closely related to your introduction? Does you conclusion bring everything to a nice ending? Look at your outline again. Do the objectives start at one point and build up to the conclusion? Don't be afraid to make changes at this point. Now look at your slides to see how well they follow your outline. I know, you have all your slides prepared! It is better to make changes at this point instead of trying to change course in the middle of your presentation, speech, or keynote. Are you finally happy with it? Great! If you have to change any of your slides, do it now.

Alpha and Omega: The beginning and the end

Just as you did when you finished writing your goal, objectives, and arguments, you should finally add your beginning and end slides. No, I am not talking about your introduction and conclusion. I am talking about the slides that you place before the introduction and after the conclusion.

I keep them simple. The first slide should contain the title of your presentation, your name, and any titles if necessary (CEO, MD, Ph.D., RN, etc.), and your affiliation or company. That is about it. You can fill in any blanks while you introduce yourself or give the person who will introduce you a card with any information you would like them to share as they introduce you. The title slide is usually on the screen as your audience enters the room.

The last slide or slides are a bit different. The very last slide should be a blank copy of your slide template. This is important because you want to end your presentation without leaving your last slide of information or a glaring white light from the projector bulb on the screen. The slide or slide immediately before the blank template slide should be the URL of your handouts if you posted them online (see the 'Handouts' paragraph below) and your name and e-mail address. The slide immediately before the URL slide usually has one word on it: 'Questions?'

Once you have created these slides, you are finished with the first draft of your presentation. You will probably think of changes as you read over and practice your presentation.

It is time to put everything together!

You now have your slides and are happy with your presentation. Your introduction is enticing, your arguments are in order and build to your conclusion in a smooth and sequential manner, and your conclusion pulls everything together in a nice, neat package. You have made your first and last slides.

Handouts

Audiences like handouts.... even if they never read them again. For most presentations I just print off a copy of my slides or post a URL where my handouts or presentation can be viewed or downloaded. Remember, you can print off several PowerPoint slides on one page. It is best to keep your handouts aside to discourage your audience from taking them beforehand. Handouts that are not readily available will also discourage people from running into the presentation room, asking for your handouts, and leaving. When people do this, I usually tell them that I don't know if I have enough and would rather have them come back after the presentation to get one if I have extras. I usually tell the audience during the introduction that I have handouts as a reward for those people willing to stick around until the end of the presentation. If you are not into wasting paper, remember you could post your handouts online and project the URL as your last slide.

Now, let's get back to the most important part of your presentation... you!

CHAPTER 7

SHOWPERSONSHIP

In this book I have discussed how you should go about outlining your goal, objectives, and arguments for your presentation. We've looked at structuring your content into an introduction, body, and conclusion, and designing your presentation slides. Now let's get to the fun part: actually presenting in front of an audience. (What did he just say?!)

Seasoned presenters or 'experts' who write books on how to present (other than yours truly that is) would probably not like the chapter title 'Showpersonship'! They might very well be screaming "No, be yourself!" But as you know already, I do not agree with the 'Be yourself' crowd. You are an actor on a stage!

PoweredPointer 28: You are an actor on a stage

I believe it all comes down to semantics. I have studied many presenters on and off stage. Most of them are different people on and off the stage. They are all acting, no matter what the presenter or the writers are saying. Most, well all, of these same seasoned presenters analyze their audience and craft their presentation to meet the needs, attitudes, language, etc. of their audience. They act in a certain way to reach their audience so they can get their point across. Those presenters are not being themselves. They are acting. How you act as you present each bullet is what changes your presentation from a list of bulleted items to a presentation where the audience connects with you and will really learn from it and enjoy it.

There are only two ideas that you have to remember to be a great presenter. The first one we have covered: your slides should contain all the points you want to get across. You have to list these points simply and concisely. Your verbal presentation is just the filler. Your verbal presentation may be a bit different each time, just like each peanut is a little different from all the other peanuts in the world however each peanut contains the essence of 'peanut' (taste, look, smell, etc.), and each of your presentations will contain the essence (information) you hope to get across.

The second idea is that you are an actor onstage. Don't be yourself.

 "Truly great speeches live in the intersection of education and theater" (McLellan, 2020).

PoweredPointer 29: You are the medium

Marshall McLuhan and Quentin Fiore first published a book called *The Medium is the Message* in 1967. In it they said that as new technologies become more integrated into our lives, the new technology changes how we sense and perceive things or, at least, that was what my ninth grade teacher told me they said. If I am wrong you will have to discuss it with Mr. Blydenburgh. You have a message. You are the medium!

When I say that you are the medium, I mean that you are the conduit through which ideas, information, and knowledge moves from a source (your brain) to the audience. But you are more than just a hollow pipe through which information passes like an echo ringing through a cave. You choose, manipulate, and showcase your information in such a way that your audience will understand the point(s) you want to get across. For example, this book is the information. You are reading my message in this book. The book is the medium and, because it is the medium, you may be interpreting what I am writing in ways that may be a little different from the interpretation that I am attempting to get across as I sit here and type, and not as I would act out the message in front of you. If I am doing a good job writing the book, the differences should be quite small. If you were to come to one of my presentations on presenting, you should have an even clearer picture of my message. I use voice, facial expressions, gestures, and body movements to illustrate and emphasize my points.

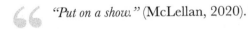 *"Put on a show."* (McLellan, 2020).

Think of the location where you will be giving your talk as your stage. Don't tie yourself down to one area of your stage. Use any part of the stage that you want. Many of the older folks remember Steve Jobs. For you younger folks, he was a founder and for most of the early years, the head of Apple Inc. He loved to introduce new products to the public. He didn't just stand behind a podium and talk during these introductions. He walked around the stage, he gestured, and people paid attention. Most of the time there was no podium on the stage.

A word of advice: Don't use a podium unless you are giving a simple speech. I never used one in my 500 plus presentations. I tried not to use one when giving keynote speeches either. The biggest problem with giving a keynote speech is using a stationary microphone. Podiums made me nervous when I stepped behind them. Use your stage: the front of the room or the front of the stage you are on. Remember, your notes are on the screen. You know what you want to say. You will be ad-libbing the rest. *Not all peanuts are the same.*

PoweredPointer 30: The room is your stage

You have a whole room: don't be afraid to use it. In the vast majority of presentations, you will just be using the front of the room. There are certain times when the back of the room will also be important. I will talk about that when I discuss setting up the room. Remember: Unless you are giving a speech with no presentation tools, try not to use a podium.

PoweredPointer 31: Keep it light

Try to keep your presentation a bit on the light side. Yes, yes, of course this depends on the topic that you are covering. I never had to worry about that in any of my presentations. You are up in front; be happy and enjoy yourself. Put a smile on your face and you will actually start to feel better and more in control. Your audience does not want to have a somber presenter. Every hear a eulogy without having a little laugh? If you have done everything that I have and will recommend, you will do a good—no, a great job! Have fun! Don't be afraid to be Jack Benny.

PoweredPointer 32: Control attention

Make sure that you are the one who controls your audience. If you don't control them, there is a chance that your audience will control you! We will discuss a number of ways to do this. When you pre-check the presentation room, you should pay particular attention to items that may cause a distraction. Try to eliminate or minimize as many of these as possible. Most presentation rooms do not have windows. If you are in one that does have windows, close the drapes or blinds. Keep the door closed to minimize distractions from the hallway. If there is a problem with sound coming in from the outside or from another room, or from a room fan that sounds like a B-25, speak to someone at the venue about eliminating it. You can't control the attention of your audience if there are distractions.

Also make sure that your visuals and sound are synchronized. It is best not to have your slides progress automatically. As I said earlier, reveal only one bullet at a time. Otherwise your audience will be copying down the next bullet, and the next, and not really paying close attention to what you are saying. This is a good reason for not handing out your handouts before the presentation, especially if they consist of a print-off of your presentation slides. Visuals and sound have to be synchronized: don't read bullet three on slide four while the audience is reading bullet two on slide five!

PoweredPointer 33: Use the stronger areas of the stage

Where you stand and how you move around the presentation area (your stage) are important. Yes, usually it is the flat floor at the front of the presentation room, though many times it could also be up on a real stage. Check out this map:

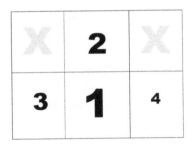

Now you are thinking: "OK, what is it?" This is a strength map for the front of the stage. The map shows you the strongest area of the stage (front and center) and the no-fly zones (the back corners). In the ideal presentation world you want to be right up there in the front and center of the room. Remember though, I said that you should move around. Just try to stay mostly in the front and center of the stage. This is called 'stage strength'. You can use stage strength to your advantage. Let's say that you have an important point to make. As you are talking before you make your important point, slowly move back near or into stage strength area two. It doesn't have to be very far back. Now, move quickly up into stage strength area one as you dramatically (more on this later) make your point. Use stage strength to your advantage. Just by doing this simple move, you are emphasizing the importance of the point you are making!

PoweredPointer 34: Try to keep the screen off to the side

I know, this is easier said than done. In most presentation rooms, the screen is attached to the ceiling in the center of the front wall. In that case, there is nothing you can do about it. If you do have the option of setting up a screen, try to set it off to the side. Either side will do. The right side is better though, since most people start to look and read from left to right and you want to be in this starting position. Just try to make sure the screen is not taking center stage away from you. Before the screen is set up, move around your stage to see which corner would work best for you. You have to consider electrical outlets, room entrances, etc. If you do have the screen in the center of the front wall, move to the side (if possible) as you reveal and read the bullets to the audience. Glance at the bullet and turn to the audience before you say it. There is no reason why you can't move back to center stage after the bullet is revealed if you are not blocking the light from the projector.

I was looking at a few videos on YouTube featuring Steve Jobs. When he was just talking, he would gravitate to the center of the stage. When he was introducing a product he would step to the side (!) and let the product take center stage on the large screen. Just as you are the most important part of your presentation, the product was the most important part of Steve's presentation!

Ok, actors to be, now let's get down to the real nitty-gritty of how you should behave in front of your audience.

PoweredPointer 35: Talk only to people, not your notes or the screen

It is really important that you talk only to the audience, unless you are writing something on a whiteboard, blackboard or flip chart. Look at the newly revealed bullet and look back at your audience before you start talking. You want everyone to hear you and see your facial expressions and observe your body language. I am sure that you have seen presenters reading the new bullet while they are looking at the bullet on the screen. What did they say? It sounded like 'mumble, mumble' to me. (Is that a bald spot on the back of his head?) Not good!

Remember, the only time you will want to read a bullet as your back is turned to the audience is when you are writing on a black/whiteboard or flip chart. Don't keep your back fully turned to the audience as you are doing this though. Try to cock your head to one side towards the audience. Most people will write along with your voice as you speak, since you will usually be blocking the words as you are speaking them anyway.

PoweredPointer 36: Work the whole room

Most of the time you will see some friendly faces in your audience. They may nod acceptance, gesture, or smile. Don't home in on those friendly faces though. You are presenting to the entire audience. Make sure each audience member feels as if you are talking to them. I volunteer at a music venue during the summer. It is surprising how many (famous) performers seem to home in on an area (stage right, stage left, down in front) and miss whole areas of the audience. This goes along with my next point.

PoweredPointer 37: Don't scan the room. Lock on to people's eyes for three to five seconds

Look at the people in your audience as you present. Look each of them in the eye, just for three to five seconds. This should be long enough for them to feel a connection with you, but not long enough for them to feel uncomfortable. There is also a second benefit to looking your audience members in the eyes. Most of us do not like to talk to large groups. By looking at each person individually, you will feel more like you are just talking to one person, even if it is only for a few fleeting seconds. This will help overcome nervousness! Remember *PoweredPointer 36*, though. Don't go down one row or section at a time. Work the entire room but don't scan; instead lock on to one person and the next, and the next. Don't believe what you have read that says that if you are nervous, look slightly above the audience and concentrate on the back wall! No, look at the individual audience members: just one at a time.

PoweredPointer 38: Use your voice to energize both your presentation and your audience

Great actors have great voices. They are able to manipulate their voices to match the mood, the script, and the situation. See if you can find an old radio show on the web or on satellite radio. Listen to it. All you are doing is hearing the actors, and yet the actors are painting a picture in your mind of where they are and what they are doing. Great actors don't just read scripts, they play them. Don't stand in front of your audience and tell them what you want them to know. Dive in to your message and bring it to life. Have expression in your voice. I am sure that you don't use a deadpan voice when talking with friends and colleagues. Vocal expression will help you keep your audience interested in what you are saying. It will involve them and it will help keep you in charge.

PoweredPointer 39: Use strong gestures to emphasize points and to 'paint images'

Don't be afraid to use strong gestures. For example, when you say something about the whole world, put your hands in front of you and spread them horizontally to the sides or move them in a large circular motion. If you say something like "think about it", hold your chin in your hand as if you are thinking. Perhaps even look puzzled or contemplative as you do this. Remember, you want to hold your audience's attention. They should have written down your bullet point first. Their eyes should subconsciously gravitate back to you when they are finished writing. Now you are explaining it. Ham it up. And smile: it relaxes everyone. *Including you!* This is not like you? It is not me either, but I do it! Work at it. You will be surprised how easy hamming it up really is. You may even start enjoying your own presentation. And more importantly; strong gestures will help you get your information across to your audience!

Let's go back to Steve Jobs. He practiced his speeches over and over again and analyzed every single gesture and every single word in his presentations. His archrival from Microsoft, Bill Gates, described Jobs as being able to cast spells over his audience (McLellan, 2020).

Let's switch to a very different type of person now. One who is far from a role model. I thought long and hard about whether I should put in the following. Unfortunately, it does really reinforce many of my points.

If you look online, I am sure that you can find a set of photographs that Heinrich Hoffmann, Adolf Hitler's personal photographer, took of the brutal dictator rehearsing facial expressions and hand gestures as he addressed an imaginary audience for one of his speeches.

"I know that men are won over less by the written than by the spoken word, that every great movement on this earth owes its growth to orators and not to great writers." (Adolf Hitler, 'Author's Preface,' *Mein Kampf*, Hitler, Murphy and Carruthers, 2011).

Hitler was not a natural speaker and wanted his gestures to have as much impact as his words. In some of the photographs he can be seen angrily frowning, pointing at the (nonexistent) audience, raising his index finger to emphasize a point, and stretching his arms with his palms open seemingly to appeal to his audience. This was done "...to give the 'showman' Führer an insight into how he looked to the German public" (Enoch, 2014; Philip, 2019). When the photographs were developed (younger people have no idea what I am talking about), Hitler would go over each one to decide which, if any, of the movements and expressions he would use. "He was an absolutely spellbinding public speaker and these pictures show that it was something he worked very hard on." (*Hitler's speech rehearsal visualized*, Moorhouse, n.d.).

PoweredPointer 40: Don't make unnecessary movements

This probably seems like a strange thing to say after *PoweredPointer 31*. It really is not. Your *every* move should have a reason. If you perform the same presentation over and over, you will even have your movements down to a pattern— almost. You will at least go over your presentation several (read that many) times before the 'big day'. Rehearse your gestures as you practice your presentation. It is not easy. Some of your gestures will be ad-libbed during your talk. This is especially true the first time through. You will probably find that it is easier to add in new gestures when there is a receptive audience in front of you. You may even change some gestures to meet the needs of different audiences.

PoweredPointer 41: Avoid putting your hands together

Please don't put your hands together unless it is part of a gesture. If you have nothing better to do with your hands, just drop them to your sides. It may feel funny just letting your hands hang there. Audience members will not even notice though. Dropping your hand is not that difficult to do and it looks more professional then fidgeting or playing with something. Later I will talk about a little trick you can do while your hands are by your sides to help ease any anxiety you may have.

PoweredPointer 42: Avoid 'toys', pointers, pocket change, jewelry, etc.

In other words, don't have anything nearby or in your pockets that you can play with. Many of us tend to fidget or play with toys when we get nervous. Keep your hands out of your pockets. Don't play with your bracelet, twist your ring, spin your pointer, and especially don't keep pulling up your socks.

PoweredPointer 43: Do what works for the audience

This is one of the most important PoweredPointers: *Do what works for the audience*—not necessarily what is comfortable for you. Your job as a presenter is to get your information across to your audience. You will have researched your audience by the time you present, so you should have a good idea of who they are and what their interests are. If you don't do your research, you may lose your audience even before you start with your presentation. Here is a little example I use when I get to this part in my presentation on doing presentations: Hold your hands out in front of you and interlock your fingers. Which thumb is on top? (My left one is.) Now, unlace your fingers and put them together with the opposite thumb on top. You will notice that this is not as 'normal' or natural for you. Perhaps you are a left lacer and your audience is filled with right lacers. If you want to get your point across with the minimum amount of distraction and discomfort to your audience you will have to right lace, even though it may not be as comfortable for you to do this.

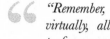 *"Remember, whether you are presenting in-person or virtually, all presentations are performances. And all performances are in service to your audience"* (Abbajay, 2020).

Do what works for the audience even if it is not your style. One more time: You have to use your knowledge to give a presentation that works for your audience.

CHAPTER 8

SHOWPERSONSHIP: QUESTIONING TECHNIQUES

Even if you had a perfect peanut: you covered everything that you wanted to, your audience feedback (nods, smiles, understanding looks) was all very positive, there usually comes a time when you ask the audience if they have any questions. This is an area that sometimes makes new presenters nervous. After all, when you open up the floor for questions you really don't have complete control anymore because now the audience members are the ones choosing the direction of the discussion. You still have to keep control though. Don't despair. Unless you have really not prepared, you will have more control over the audience than you think.

PoweredPointer 44: Indicate in the introduction that you would like the audience to hold their questions until the end of the presentation

Some presenters let their audience ask questions throughout their presentations. I rarely do this and believe that you should follow my lead. This, of course, ultimately depends on the subject you are covering though. In some circumstances, questions during a presentation may be expected. You may even include questions and discussions with your presentation. This is particularly important during virtual presentations since it is much more difficult to read your audience to see if they understand you. Questions and discussions also involve them and helps to keep their interest up. In either case, you should take questions into consideration as you are designing your presentation.

You do have specific points that you need to cover in a specific period of time. You have practiced and practiced, and after that you practiced some more. You really don't need to be bogged down by questions throughout your performance. Besides, if you prepared your performance (OK: presentation) correctly and used your audience research, there should be little need for questions until the end. Every point should build on the previous one. If, for some reason, you do see a multitude of puzzled looks on the faces in your audience, you can just go right ahead and give more examples or re-explain your point in a different way. It is a two-way street: your audience pays attention to you and you have to pay attention to your audience. We are not perfect, and even the most seasoned presenter misses the boat sometimes. You may get someone who stops you and asks you to explain or re-explain a point. Or you may see quizzical looks in your audience or people whispering to each other. Again, if this happens you should stop and re-explain your point. You don't want to lose your audience.

PoweredPointer 45: Ask if there are any questions with a raised hand

You have reached the end of your presentation. It is now time for the question and answer period. Don't just say: "Any questions?" or "Let's open it up for a few questions now." Rather pause, *raise your hand,* and say "Are there any questions now?" Just by raising your hand you have shown your audience what you expect from them. It is surprising how this one little action can change the whole tone of the question and answer session. You should always be in control, from the beginning of your presentation through to the very end when you sit down or walk out the door.

PoweredPointer 46: Point to the questioner with an open hand

Many presenters point at the person they would like to have ask a question. Others just look at the person and nod. When was the last time someone looked directly at you, pointed a finger at you, and asked you something? I am sure that it was not your significant other or your mother saying something nice. Why do you point at an audience member? Ask for questions while you raise your hand, look at the person you would like to ask a question, gesture to them with an open hand (like offering them your hand in a hand shake), and listen to their question. When I am giving a presentation on how to give presentations, I usually move my hand from left to right and say something like: "And if you don't like the question, you will be one step closer to slapping the questioner upside of the head." (Audience laughter usually follows… usually. Especially if you say it with a straight face!)

PoweredPointer 47: Avoid using names unless you know everyone in the room

I am sure that you have been at presentations where the presenter knows many of the audience members and calls on them by name and/or makes some comment to or about them during or after the presentation. All well and good if there is a famous person, someone you need to thank, or an expert in the audience that you would like to recognize. Aside from that, try to avoid using names. It makes some people feel left out and/or not part of the group. If you know that you will know most people in the room and you notice a new face, introduce yourself as you talk to audience members before your presentation begins and try to remember, or better yet, jot down their name. In this way you will be better able to use names and be more inclusive with your audience.

PoweredPointer 48: After the question is asked, break visual contact with the questioner and repeat or rephrase the question to the audience

How many times have you attended a presentation when a question was asked that you were not able to hear or perhaps understand? Or you heard something but whispered "What did they say?" to your neighbor? This is the reason you break visual contact with the questioner, look at the audience, and repeat or rephrase the question. Doing this does a number of things: 1. It allows the questioner to hear the question and correct you if you misheard it; 2. It affords you the opportunity to make sure that everyone in the audience heard the question; 3. It allows you to include the audience in the question and subsequent discussion; 4. It allows you a few moments to collect your thoughts and prepare what you are going to say; 5. It allows you to better able deflect a hostile questioner. *"What does a someone in a cheap suit who has never done 'x' know about (firefighting, baking, computer programing…)?"* = *"The gentleman is asking me about my qualifications."*

PoweredPointer 49: Do not preface your answer

At news conferences and on talk shows politicians preface their answers, usually because they want to get a different point across (think presidential debates), don't want to answer the question (think presidential debates), or don't know the answer (and once again…). You are (in theory) the expert on your topic and usually the questions are about something that was in your presentation. Don't be afraid to admit when you don't know the answer. You may want to turn the question back to the audience. Many times someone in attendance will know the answer. If no one can, tell the questioner and audience that you will try to find out and email them the answer.

PoweredPointer 50: Employ the 25% − 75% eye contact rule

Remember, you are giving the presentation to the whole audience. You should also be answering questions for the whole audience to hear. I am sure that you have sat in presentations where someone asks a question (that you can't or didn't hear) and the presenter and the questioner have a grand old time talking to each other about the answer. Two-way conversations like this are isolated occurrences. . The best way not to get caught in this is to spend about 25% of the time talking to the questioner and about 75% of the time talking to the rest of the audience, everyone hears you and feels included in the conversation. I should have called this 'Don's eye contact rule'. Remember to try to cover the whole room and to look each audience member in the eye for three to five seconds as you respond to the question. Several public speaking coaches suggest that you look away from the questioner as you finish answering their question (Miller, 2016). This helps prevent follow-up questions by the same individual (think presidential press conferences). This is especially important if you have many audience members who have questions. You can always return to that person if time permits. I usually want to know if I have answered the question, so I don't look away.

PoweredPointer 51: Prepare for questions ahead of time

After you have finished preparing your presentation, go through it a few times and try to think about questions that people might ask. This is not easy. If you thought that it would be a question, you probably would have covered it in your presentation. Even so, try to prepare some questions in advance. You don't want to be caught looking at an audience after the presentation and having them look like deer caught in headlights when you ask if they have any questions. If this does happen though, start by saying "Here is a question that is sometimes asked…" This is a good place to add another point, or to clarify or enhance information you talked about earlier. This is a perfect time to add anything you forgot to include earlier in your presentation. You should always have enough background information and knowledge on the topic to explain or further enhance any point that you are going to make in your presentation.

CHAPTER 9

SHOWPERSONSHIP: REDUCING ANXIETY

> *"I'm always just very nervous. I never feel like, 'I've got this'."* – Jennifer Lawrence, actress with one Oscar, 118 other award wins and 177 award nominations (Hickson, 2016).

> *"I have stage fright every single concert I've ever done. I have at least four or five minutes of it. It's absolute living hell."* Brian Wilson, singer/songwriter of the Beach Boys, with six awards and nine award nominations (BrainyQuotes, n.d.)

> *"If you get stage fright, it never goes away. But then I wonder: is the key to that magical performance because of fear?"* – Stevie Nicks, singer/producer with over 40 top-50 hits and who has sold over 140 million recordings with Fleetwood Mac (British music group) with six awards and nine award nominations (AZ Quotes, n.d.)

"Surveys about our fears commonly show fear of public speaking at the top of the list," states Dr. Glenn Croston in an article on the *Psychology Today* website (Croston, 2012). There is even a name for the fear of public speaking: glossophobia (*glossa* meaning tongue and *phobos* meaning fear or dread) more commonly known as speech anxiety. The comments by many other psychologists echo the same thing.

A public speaking blog cited a survey of 1000 people in the Spring 1987 issue of *Dental Health Advisor* magazine (Garber, 2012). (How many people talk in front of an audience as they are getting their teeth cleaned? I don't think that fears of public speaking would be my number-one fear while in a dentist's chair!) I also found another citation in an older paper by Dr. Karen Kangas Dwyer and Marlina M. Davidson attributing public speaking as the number-one fear to a 1973 'R.H. Bruskin Associates' American Fears' study that appeared in the *London Times*. Both of the studies came to the same conclusion (Dwyer & Davidson, 2012). Also, both studies found that 'Speaking before a group' ranked not only number one but also ranked higher than the fear of death! In the Bruskin Associates study, death came in at number seven; in the Dwyer and Davidson study, death was the number-three fear!

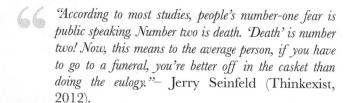

"According to most studies, people's number-one fear is public speaking. Number two is death. 'Death' is number two! Now, this means to the average person, if you have to go to a funeral, you're better off in the casket than doing the eulogy."– Jerry Seinfeld (Thinkexist, 2012).

PoweredPointer 52: People would rather be dead than speak in public

At this point, it is not relevant how anyone else feels. You will be the one speaking in front of an audience—period. You have no choice. Perhaps knowing that almost everyone in your positions feels the same way will help, although that thought never helped me. It never gave me comfort to think that most people would not want to be in my shoes as I waited to do my presentation! It may comfort you to know that 99.999999% of speakers/presenters don't fall over dead onstage, get booed off the stage, or totally screw up their presentation or speech. I will say this again later: As long as you just correct mistakes as you become aware of them and don't make a big deal out of any mistakes you do make (We ALL make mistakes), most people will not even realize that you made one. And besides, the audience is on your side and will usually just gloss over any problems. Someone once said you can think of presenting like childbirth. Most people (in this case women) are not looking forward to the actual process but when it is over, the outcome is worth it.

Why are people so afraid of public speaking? Below is a list I picked up several years ago describing the reasons people do not want to speak before a group.

- *37% feel that they will be unable to answer questions.* Remember we talked about questioning technique in the last chapter? Unless you are going to talk about something you really know nothing about, *and/or* you really did not take the time to prepare your presentation, questions should not be a problem. Of course, many presenters have been faced with a difficult question at one time or another. If this happens to you, just be honest and say that it is a great question but you really don't know the answer. It is as simple as that! You could tell the questioner you will find out and email them, and (even better) ask if anyone in the audience can help with the answer.
- *45% are afraid of being stared at.* Just remember, you will not be talking to the group but to the individuals in the group. Besides, you may be keeping your audience too busy taking notes to stare at you.
- *77% are afraid they may damage their career or reputation* (if you are prepared, you won't do this); freeze up or be unable to speak (if you are prepared and

study this section you won't have to worry about that); or bore their listeners (if you play it the way I say it, your audience will not be bored!).

- *81% are afraid that they will make embarrassing mistakes.*

And down the list:

- *31% fear that they will be unprepared.* (How can that be? Don't worry; you will be prepared!)
- *24% fear being ignored; 19% being laughed at; 7% that the audience will fall asleep.* (I just wonder who was surveyed to get these numbers. If this happens to you, just leave!)

———

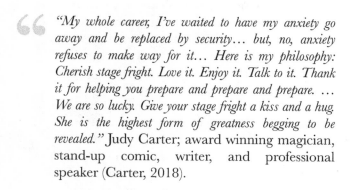

"My whole career, I've waited to have my anxiety go away and be replaced by security… but, no, anxiety refuses to make way for it… Here is my philosophy: Cherish stage fright. Love it. Enjoy it. Talk to it. Thank it for helping you prepare and prepare and prepare. … We are so lucky. Give your stage fright a kiss and a hug. She is the highest form of greatness begging to be revealed." Judy Carter; award winning magician, stand-up comic, writer, and professional speaker (Carter, 2018).

Reframe your fears. Turn your fears into excitement! Don't dwell on being nervous. Change you nerves into the excitement you have being able to present new or different information to you audience.

"Courage is resistance to fear, mastery of fear — not absence of fear." – Mark Twain (Thorpe, 2014).

OK. Let's get right down to different techniques you can make use of to reduce anxiety. Remember "…95% of the success of your presentation is determined before you present" (Kettenhofen, 2006).

PoweredPointer 53: Organize your material

Wow, that should be easy. You have already done that. After you have finished preparing and completing many rehearsals, arrange all of your notes, handouts, and other material in order and put them all aside. Also gather any other material you may need before, during, and after your presentation. Do all of this as early as you can. Things always come up, so no last-minute preparation please! I have a small travel clock I always take with me since many rooms don't have clocks and it keeps me from glancing at my watch. I also take a few containers of candy like Tic Tacs. You may want to grab a water bottle just in case: some rooms don't have water available in the back. It is easy to do all of this at home or in the office (again well) before the presentation. Since you may have an idea of the type of room you are presenting in, think of anything else you may need. It is always better to be over-prepared! This includes an extra copy of your presentation on a thumb drive and perhaps even an extension cord! In Chapter 10 we will talk about everything I gather as I am preparing for my presentation.

PoweredPointer 54: Visualize your presentation

Try to find a room where you can be alone so you can rehearse your presentation *without any distractions*. It would be nice to have a room with a desk or table in it. Set everything up the way you hope it will be in your actual presentation room and run through your presentation from the very beginning to the very end. Start from the *very* beginning. Stand aside as you visualize someone introducing you. Walk to the middle (center stage), thank them, and jump right in. Visualize an audience sitting in front of you. I personally don't like to stand around and let someone introduce me. I tell the room monitor that I would rather do it myself. Most room monitors are very happy not to have to say anything (Is this because *they* fear speaking in public?!) You know me by now: by introducing myself I don't have to stand up in front of everyone and be 'pointed out'.

PoweredPointer 55: Practice, practice, practice

I can't say this enough: practice. Practice will give you a chance to fill out what you want to say as you reveal each of the bullets in your visuals. Remember the peanut. *Do not* memorize your presentation. If you do and you forget what comes next, you may panic. You will use each bullet on your presentation as a starting point to fill in and smooth the path to your next bullet or thought. The more you practice, the easier it will be to cover all the material you want to cover. Your bullets are the essence of your presentation: the information you want to get across. Everyone will see, hear, and hopefully process each one. Your actual words will vary with each presentation though.

Practice, practice, practice. Again, I am talking about practicing the whole presentation from being introduced through to your saying *thank you* (or whatever) at the end. This is also the time you should add humor, pauses, gestures, mannerisms, etc. Someone looking into the room where you are practicing will think you have an audience (or are nuts). If you can't record your practice sessions, see if you can ask a friend to sit in. Ask them to pay particular attention to any quirks you have when you present. Do you say "right", "OK", or something else before every pause? Do you shift your weight from side to side? Do you move your ring around on your finger? Practice is also the key to reducing anxiety and stage fright. "Studies show that by rehearsing and truly being prepared, you can reduce nervousness by 75%" (Kettenhofen, 2006).

Don't be afraid to try new ideas as you go along. Several years ago there was a series of commercials on the radio for a motel chain. The very last words spoken by the announcer were, "we'll keep the light on for you". Was it written in that first commercial's script? Not at all. During the production of the commercial the announcer had a few seconds left over and rather than have dead air at the end, he simply added the phrase. "We'll keep the light on for you" became a marketing slogan for the motel chain and it was added onto the end of all of their commercials for several years. There are websites that list famous movie dialogue that was ad-libbed by the actor during filming and kept in the movie when it was released!

In mid 2020 Microsoft came out with a great enhancement to PowerPoint in Office 365 called 'Presenter Coach'. This is an interesting AI tool that helps you as you rehearse your presentation. It can actually evaluate pitch, euphemisms, pacing, culturally sensitive terms, if you use filler words, and even informal speech in your presentation (Microsoft, 2019).

PoweredPointer 56: Deep breaths before you go on will help you relax

I am sure that you have heard of the 'fight or flight' response. This is also known as the 'stress response'. It is a physiological response that kicks in automatically when we are faced with a situation that we perceive to be physically or mentally dangerous or harmful. It is the body's way to prepare us to deal with a danger head-on (fight) or to turn tail and run away (flight). Some of the physical signs of the stress response include dilated pupils, flushed or pale skin (blood is diverted to the brain and muscles), rapid heartbeat and breathing (for more rapid energy utilization), and trembling (as your muscles become primed for action). This is a great response if you have to fight or run. This is not a great response if you are trying to give a presentation.

I bet that most of you did not know that there is also a 'relaxation response'. There are many ways to evoke this response: yoga, meditation, prayer, and progressive muscle relaxation are just a few. Another way to draw out the relaxation response is through focused deep breathing (Harvard Health, 2015). Brain scans have actually shown that slow, deep, and meditative breathing can reduce brain and nervous system stress levels dramatically (Newlyn, 2019). Many speakers use this technique. I had heard about this technique several times but it really hit home for me when I was at a presentation by a nationally known individual in Rochester, Minnesota. As he was being introduced he stood at the side of the stage doing focused deep breathing! Over the years, I have noticed other 'professionals' using this same technique before a presentation or speech.

Focused deep breathing is really very simple. Just stop what you are doing, sit or stand up straight, and slowly breath in deeply to the count of five, hold your breath for five more counts, and exhale for five counts. Now, repeat this again. If you are doing this correctly, your lower belly will rise. Stop reading for a few moments and try practicing focused deep breathing for yourself. You should feel less tense.

PoweredPointer 57: Focus on relaxing

Before you go out on stage, stop and focus your thoughts and your body on relaxing. Try these simple steps: 1. Stand with your arms at your side (or sit comfortably). 2. Put your head slightly down and close your eyes. 3. Breathe slowly as you think about the movement of your lungs and chest. 4. Repeat something like "I am going to knock this presentation out of the park" several times.

PoweredPointer 58: Release tension with isometric exercises

This is a simple trick that research shows really works. Drop a hand to your side and form an 'OK' sign with your thumb and index (pointing) finger. Now all you have to do is press these fingers together. That is it. Try it. It really will help reduce tension!

PoweredPointer 59: Get to know the audience

You have done your audience research. You know some-thing about their age, demographics, job, why they are at your presentation, and other details about them—at least on paper. Now it is time to connect your knowledge with the real people who will be your audience. Your performance (presen-tation) is not a play, so don't stay behind the curtain or off to the side as the audience comes in. By the time the audience starts to enter the venue, you should already have the room and your presentation set up the way you want it. (Perhaps I should have started that sentence with 'In a perfect world…'.) Many times you have 15 minutes to get the previous person out of the way and your presentation set up. Still, try to circu-late or at least talk with several different audience members before you start your 'show'. Now is the time to circulate, introduce yourself, talk to people and find out a little about them. The more people you can talk with, the better. Smile, enjoy, make connections. It is better to be able to talk with them when they are in the room. If you hover by the door they might just walk by or be pushed into the room by the gathering masses. You may pick up some hints that could help you fill in your discussion and/or change some of the emphasis or direction of your presentation. Bonding with the members of the audience is important. Most of them will feel flattered that you are talking with them. If you don't have time to do this, don't worry; you are well prepared and will do great!

PoweredPointer 60: Maintain eye contact with your audience

It is much easier to talk to one person than it is to talk to a crowd. How do we do this with a large group of happy faces in front of us? Think of the audience members as individuals. Yes, we have said this all before but it does bear repeating. You probably met some or many of them earlier. Individual eye contact is the key. Look directly into the eyes of your audience members as you present. Don't keep eye contact with one person for very long though. Three to five seconds should be enough before you move on to another person. And don't just go down one row after another. Skip around and be sure to cover all the areas in the room. In this way you will be making individuals in each area feel important and you will be keeping audience members on their toes. You will not be speaking to a crowd, just individual members of your audience. Just remember to talk to one person at a time, then another person, and then another person. Just remember: one person at a time. See, you feel more relaxed already! Three to five seconds will help you connect with your audience members but it is not long enough to make them feel uneasy. The last thing you want is a creeped out audience sitting in front of you. They may not stick around for long.

PoweredPointer 61: Reduce or cut out coffee consumption

I love coffee. I cannot ever remember not drinking coffee. My earliest memory of breakfast as a little kid is having just toast and coffee. (I am sure if this were today my mother would be arrested and charged with child endangerment!) Coffee and all caffeinated drinks can be a problem though. Remember that you start your presentation well before you actually walk into the room. Your presentation started weeks ago when you first said "yes" and does not end until you have evaluated your presentation perhaps a few days later. But the day or days just before you present are still make-or-break days. Some of the bits and pieces you must take into consideration at this time are sleep, food, and drink. You must eat and drink wisely. Caffeinated drinks can make you nervous and make you want to pee.

Limit your fluid intake before you present. You never can tell when or even if you will have time to go to a toilet. Even if your presentation location is close to a toilet, when you really need it there could be lines there or it could be a very inopportune time for the venue staff to be cleaning it. You never can tell. Back to coffee and caffeinated drinks. If you are really addicted to caffeine, have one cup of coffee and strengthen it with a teaspoon of instant. Remember though, some research has found that caffeinated drinks like coffee, tea, and soda are dehydrating (Frisbee, 2019; Salinas, 2017). While I am at it I might as well mention that alcohol also is dehydrating (Wilkinson, n.d.). The last thing we need is a dry mouth when we are presenting!

I am sure that you will place water glasses or bottles in several places nearby your presentation spot. I try to place two or three bottles or glasses around the front of the room so there will always be one handy between bullets. Another trick I have learned is to have small candies available in several places around the room and in my pockets. I use Tic Tacs. I have said that several times, but I promise that I have no commercial interest in the company! Just pop one in your mouth and slide it under your tongue. You should generate enough saliva to keep going and not have to worry about going (to the toilet).

PoweredPointer 62: Reduce foods that contain cholesterol and fat

Years ago I read that foods containing cholesterol and fat dry out your mouth (not something you want when you present.) I put that in my 'better safe than sorry' file. About five years ago I was sitting in a presentation by a medical doctor and lo and behold he actually said the same thing! I usually limit my eating preceding a presentation. This is not easy if you are scheduled to present directly after a meal. I do keep snacks available just in case. Better to hear my voice than my stomach! I chow down afterwards.

You may also have dry mouth because of the medications you are taking. Dry mouth is a common side effect of many prescription medications for diabetes, high blood pressure, heart disease, and high cholesterol along with cold medications, antihistamines, antidepressants, and antipsychotics. I guess that physiology works against older people when it comes to presenting. It is a good idea to stay away from too much salt and salty foods as well. Make sure you keep water and Tic Tacs handy! Review *PoweredGuide 9: Reducing Anxiety* in Appendix 2 before your presentation.

Find a nice quiet area where you will not be disturbed and set up your equipment just as you might do in your future presentation room. Pretend the room is full, and start your presentation from the very beginning. By starting from the very beginning I mean from standing to the side as a non-existent moderator introduces you. Or you could just walk right out and introduce yourself as I like to do. With enough repetition, most—if not all—of your supplemental material will be incorporated into your presentation. Practice revealing one bullet at a time and fill in any of the associated information right after. Don't forget to read each bullet aloud and pause after you read it to give the (nonexistent) audience time to write it down. Your basic presentation is the collection of bullets you wrote. You may not describe each one exactly the same way each time you give the presentation to your empty or full room. You will convey most of what you want to get across to the audience though. If you forget something important, it will probably come to you later on. At that point, jot it down so you can incorporate it into your next run-through. If this happens when you are actually in front of a live audience, you can always tell them at that time, add it later at a more appropriate time, or add the information to the end of your presentation. After you have done this a few times, invite a friend or colleague to sit in and critique your presentation. See *PoweredGuide 9: Rehearsal Checklist and Comments* in Appendix 2 for a handy guide to help your friends and colleagues critique your presentation.

Now let's discuss the actual day of your presentation. The following chapter will review and discuss what to expect and what you should be doing on the day to prepare. The last chapter is a little review that will help you pull any loose ends together. Several readers have told me that they reread the last two chapters again closer to the big day just to make sure they are prepared. You should still have plenty of time to think about all that I have written.

CHAPTER 10

THE BIG DAY!

The big day has finally arrived. You have practiced your presentation many, many (did I say many?) times. You should be all set to go. Remember what Kettenhofen (2006) found: First, if you have rehearsed and are truly prepared, nervousness can be reduced by 75%; and second, 95% of presentation success is determined before you actually present. Preparation is the key to both a lower level of stress and a successful presentation!

PoweredPointer 63: Preparation will reduce stress and greatly enhance presentation success

Set aside a bag/box/container to put your materials in. I call it my 'prep bag', although it could be several bags or boxes or containers. Take some time to make sure that your 'prep bag' has everything in it you will need to take with you. Set up your 'prep bag' a few weeks before you are to present. Things happen and time flies so don't leave anything until the last minute (or even the last week)! Of course, if you are presenting to the meat packers and have five pounds of ground beef to use in a demonstration, you probably want to put it in the refrigerator. If that is the case though, put a note in your prep box to remind you to remember it!

Here are some items that I find handy to include in my 'prep bag': small hard candies to help keep your mouth moist (Tic Tacs are great), a travel alarm clock, a disposable water bottle, your presentation, extra copies of your presentation (jump drives also called USB sticks or thumb drives) are great for this), a paper copy of your presentation (for review before you go on—just in case...), handouts or a URL where you have or will post your handouts, a computer (does the venue supply one or can/do you use your own computer?), any wires or connections you may need (an extension cord?), and any other items you think that you will need. See *PoweredGuide 4: Your Prep Bag* in Appendix 2 for a handy guide to help you fill your prep bag.

Arrive at the venue before your time to present and check out the room where you will be presenting. Do this even if you don't present for a day or two. Double-check that the room printed in the program or the room you expect to be in is really the room assigned to you. This is really important. Changes do occur. Again, if you are not going to present for a few days, you should still check your assigned room when you get there and several times throughout the conference. I usually do this several times during a conference since room configurations may change as presentations and venue needs evolve.

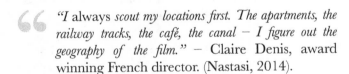

"I always scout my locations first. The apartments, the railway tracks, the café, the canal – I figure out the geography of the film." – Claire Denis, award winning French director. (Nastasi, 2014).

What furniture will be in the room and how will it be arranged? Will the venue supply a computer or can you use your own? Most venues expect you to use your own computer. If so, check to see if you have all the wiring and are able to connect the computer to the projector. Many venues have an equipment or speaker's room that might be able to help you with this. DO NOT depend on someone else for any of the items you may need. It is always better to be safe as they say! Look around the room. Where are the light switches, electrical outlets (they could be on the floor), and the exits? Are there other doors in the room and if so, where do they lead? Will you be using a microphone? Is it clip-on or stationary? If the room has windows, what about window coverings? You will probably get some information about your presentation at the registration table or at least the registration table should be able to point you in the right direction to get this information. Many presenters will be newbies so don't be afraid to ask questions. Even after hundreds of presentations I still asked questions and for help. There is no such thing as a stupid question. Most people are flattered to help. But remember that it sometimes gets a bit hectic for technical support during a conference. Is there technical support available? How do you contact them? Talk with other participants to get a feel for the attendees. See *PoweredGuide 5: Arrival Checklist* in Appendix 2 for a handy guide to help you with this.

Get a good night's sleep before the presentation. I guess that is easier said than done. Try to keep your regular schedule and remember: Even if this is your very first presentation, speech or keynote, if you follow my instructions you *WILL* knock them dead!

PoweredPointer 64: You are well prepared and will do just fine!

The day has come. Get up, clean up, and prepare yourself for the day. Do a quick check of your container (prep bag) just to make sure everything is available.

If you have not looked over your presentation room yet today, head over early to have a look if possible. Where is the nearest bathroom? (And were is the second nearest bathroom?)

Has anything changed since you saw your presentation room last? How is the furniture arranged? Do you need to make any changes? If it is a very large room and you don't expect a large crowd, you may want to tape off the last several rows. This will force the audience to move up to the front. You or the room moderator can always remove some of the tape from front to back as the audience expands. This is a very common practice among experienced presenters.

Look at the area where you will be presenting. Will the table or podium fit everything you need? Are there any tripping hazards? Make sure that you can connect your computer to their projection system. Will you need an extension cord or special wires?

Once you are happy with your ability to present your information, it is time to think about your comfort. If you can move around the front of the room, place several glasses or containers of water around the area. Also place a few Tic Tacs in each area and in a pocket if you have one. Please guys, coat pocket: not in your pants pocket! I have watched several presenters dry up in front of an audience and sometimes the audience has just watched painfully and not even offered a glass of water to them. Now, place your clock where you can glance at it and hopefully where the audience can't see its face.

You want to be ready for the audience when they start to enter the room. This is not always easy. Many times the previous presenter will still be answering questions. Don't be afraid to ask him to "clean up" his material so you can set up yours. I have had to ask that of previous presenters many times. Also, remember to 'clean up' your presentation right after you are finished. There is no reason that you can't clean up as you talk and still answer questions after your own presentation.

After you have set up your presentation and arranged your notes, candy and water, it is time to go out in the audience and meet people. Try to stop and talk with several. Ask them who they are, where they are from, and what they hope to learn. I have listed a series of questions in *PoweredGuide 7: Meeting Your Audience* in Appendix 2. You may tease out some worthwhile information and remember what I said about anxiety. (Having friendly faces in the audience will also help reduce anxiety.) If someone comes up and says that they really want to see your presentation but have another obligation (or some such story) and want a set of your handouts (if you have any), I always say that I may not have enough and would be happy to give them a set if they come back after the presentation or perhaps see me later.

Depending on when you present and your physical well-being, decide where and what you will eat. If you are presenting after lunch or dinner, remember to moderate your food/liquid/caffeine/alcohol intake. And make sure that your teeth are clean!! I usually skip the meal if I am presenting soon after. If you are presenting right after a meal, the room will probably be available for you to get into early when others are eating. Do have a granola or energy bar in your prep bag. I try to make sure that I eat something soon after my presentation.

Time your bathroom breaks. And again, are your teeth clean? No garlic on your breath?

Ready or not, here you go. (I am sure that you are ready!) You know the material, you have your presentation set, and you have the room set. You are in command!! Now it is time to get your show on the road. I said earlier that I always tell the room moderator that I will introduce myself. I think that it is easier that way. I don't have to stand around looking dumb as someone mispronounces my name and reads off my qualifications. Most moderators are very happy to have you do this. Just remember to keep it short, include some small details about yourself, limit your thank-yous, and start right in. (Bonanno, 2017). I have added several ideas designed to help the moderator introduce a presenter or to give you ideas of what to say. You may also want to read Morgan (2011) for more ideas. I have listed some of these ideas in *PoweredGuide 6: Who am I?* in Appendix 2.

Your visual presentation is your framework. All you will be doing is filling it in. You will forget some things and remember others even if you have done the same presentation before. If you are lucky enough to have a presentation you can take on the road (that is a good thing), after a while you will even have your mannerisms mastered perfectly. I think that you will feel really great after you finish. And I am sure that you will have some "I should have done this or that differently" moments. We all say that. Don't worry, it is over.

CHAPTER 11

VIRTUAL MEETINGS, VIDEOCONFERENCING, AND WEBINARS

Many things have changed since early 2020 when the world was turned upside down by Covid-19. Much of the face-to-face world has migrated to face-to-technology-to-face. This change has affected all areas of our lives. My wife attended a Zoom exercise class three times a week. A friend of mine in Massachusetts even attended a Zoom graveside funeral service for his cousin in Virginia! And, of course, most conferences and business meetings migrated to a virtual format.

So far the emphasis of this book has been on face-to-face presentations. Now we will change our focus to virtual presentations and meetings. Luckily, most of what we discussed in the earlier chapters is equally relevant to virtual presentations as well. You just have to modify a few components you learned, and you will be set to move fairly easily into the virtual world. You still have to dress nicely (at least from the neck up), and your in-person visual presentation should work just as well on a virtual platform. You will still be an actor. You will just have a very small stage!

Over the years I have taught many classes using the Internet and interactive television or virtual conferencing. I have also taught classes on how to teach over both of these mediums. I designed many Internet-based courses and have taken several online courses as well (I hated them!) To me, the transition from a physical to a virtual presentation medium was not difficult at all. If you have done regular presentations, I think you will also find this is true.

There are however some major differences that you have to look out for as you move from face-to-face meetings and presentations to virtual meetings and presentations. In this chapter we will cover the dos and don'ts of virtual meetings and presentations and highlight problems and techniques that I, along with a number of other experts, have found. We will also discuss online etiquette and review pitfalls that could hamper your success or perhaps even doom your presentation altogether. Ready? Let's jump right in!

Platforms, platforms, platforms!

The software you will be using for your virtual experience is usually referred to as a platform. The platform you use may be one of your biggest obstacles because you may not have much choice in which one you use. Lucky for you, online presentation platforms are all very similar, but unfortunately, the differences between them could also range from few to many. If you are going to be using a platform you are not familiar with, I would suggest that you first go to YouTube and/or Google to see what you can find out about the platform in question. Use search terms like "How to use…", Using…", Introduction to…", "… review", etc. Also, go to the platform's website. Most platform websites have great videos, tutorials, and helpful 'How to" information. Next, ask for help. Go to any introductory meetings of your group, association, or company, and talk with other users and your IT department about the platform. It is usually a good idea to do your own research first so you have a basic knowledge of the platform before someone else demonstrates or talks to you about it. I say this because it will usually be easier for you to grasp what they are saying if you already have some basic knowledge and familiarity with the platform. You will also be ready to ask any questions or discuss any concerns you may have discovered in your own research.

I'm not going to focus on one particular platform in this book because there are so many out there. Some of the popular ones at the time of writing are Microsoft Teams, GoToMeeting, Zoom, LoopUp, StartMeeting, Skype, ConexED, Samepage, and Google Meet. And I have not even scratched the surface of what is out there! Many companies use multiple platforms depending on the presentation or meeting needs. For example, GoToMeeting has a suite of online meeting tools including GoToConnect, GoToRoom, GoToWebinar, and GoToTraining. There are many more free and paid virtual meeting platforms available. In August of 2020, TrustRadius (2020) reviewed 91 of them! This trend reminds me of when online teaching first took hold. There must have been at least as many as 30 online teaching platforms each vying for a chance to be chosen as the gold standard. The one our university chose at the time disappeared in about 14 months. Most of the others soon went down the same drain. Luckily, much of what we will cover here will make you a better presenter regardless of the software you use.

If you are running a meeting where you can choose the platform, you may want to do a little research on your own regarding the platform's audio and video quality and mobility (devices supported, collaborative features and security, etc.). Zoom, the platform of choice at the height of the Covid-19 shutdown in mid-2020, was found to have many security gaps and holes (Feldman, 2020). With 300 million Zoom meeting participants in April 2020 alone, this could have triggered a real security headache for many industries and governments. Many businesses and government agencies were quick to restrict or even ban Zoom altogether, including Google, SpaceX, Tesla, NASA, the German Foreign Ministry, the United States Military, Taiwan, the New York City Department of Education, and the Indian government. Since new problems crop up all the time, spend a few minutes checking the platform you will be using.

In-person vs. virtual presentations

There are many similarities between in-person and virtual presentations. But there are also several differences, one of which is *not* the size of your audience. Even though it is only possible for you to view up to 49 participants on your computer screen, it is possible to have 1000 audience participants watching you during your online presentation!

Let's take a look at some other important considerations.

Holding your audience's attention

The biggest challenge you will likely face during your online presentation is keeping the audience involved. This is very important for you to be better able to hold their attention. It will also help you better understand what your audience is feeling and thinking while you present.

 "The truth is even though I've done an awful lot of zooming, it's different because you don't get the vibes." —United States Secretary of State (1997– 2001), Madeleine Albright, May 2020 (Uose, 2020).

Research has shown that virtual audiences tend to have a shorter attention span than face-to-face audiences (AMA, 2019). Other research found that the average *focused* attention span of an adult in a virtual environment is between 4 to 5 minutes (Hansen, 2020). When listening to the same presenter (that is you), a virtual audience will start to lose *all* attention after about 10 minutes. Yikes, 10 minutes does not give us much time! What can we do? We have to break our presentation down into segments that last 10 minutes or less, at which time you should insert something to engage your audience to hopefully get their attention back and to keep them involved.

PoweredPointer 65: Holding your audience's attention is your number-one goal

There are many techniques you could incorporate to hold your audience's attention, such as asking questions (can you make them quirky or unique?), playing a game, role-playing, giving the audience problems to solve, or taking a pole or a survey. This is why it's so important to know the capabilities of the platform you are using! I am sure you can think of other ways... and there is always Google! Again, remember you may have to add an attention-getter every five to 10 minutes.

Use personal language as if you are just talking to one person; a friend

Don't say something like "Is *everybody* (ready, comfortable, in the right room, etc.)?" Instead say, "Are *you* (ready, etc.)? Not "Can *everyone* hear me?" but, "Can *you* hear me?" It seems like a very small difference, but it does carry a subconscious message to your audience members. If you are addressing a virtual team make sure you use say the more inclusive "*we*" whenever possible.

Again, your biggest job is to keep your audience interested. Human beings are social creatures, and audience members may feel as strange as you may feel carrying on a dialog with a computer, television screen, or even an image projected on a much larger screen. Both you and your audience want to have a dialog with a real person and not with a machine.

 "Video lectures leave students cold. Better to have personalized, interactive courses." (Kessler, 2020).

Little things can also help hold your audience's attention

For example, many presentation platforms allow you to scribble on your slides. Do this if you can! In a face-to-face presentation you would be moving around and pointing to items on the screen. Not so in an online meeting. The scribbling movement on a static screen will bring this movement back and actually hold your audience's interest longer than no movement at all (Phuse, n.d.). This is just one example of what some platforms can do. Again, it is very important for you to know as many of the 'little tricks' available to you on the platform you are using.

Be aware of the camera problem

The camera is a barrier between you and your audience, and you have to do your best to overcome it. There are several ways to do this. One is through eye contact. Look at the camera as much as possible and not at the people on the monitor or computer. On most computers the camera is in the center of the top frame. On others it may be at the side. Play to the camera. You should also talk with your audience and not at them. They have to feel like they are a part of your presentation. Eye contact is a great help here.

There is a downside to this, though. We build trust with an audience through our eye contact and body language. Unfortunately though, a large face on a screen looking right at audience members can really unnerve some people. In one research study, a flight-or-fight or high-alert response was elicited when a researcher stared directly into a subject's eyes from two feet away (Morris, 2020). Think about how you would feel if the computer in front of you had just a face staring directly at you all the time.

"All these faces can cause enough stress in our brains to trigger a fight-or-flight response. When a barrage of large faces continually populate the screen... our brain interprets those faces as being physically close to ours— and research shows we tend to recoil from those virtual faces." (Volpe, 2020)

Looking down at the camera and lighting from a low angle will make even thin people look like they have a double chin. Alan Matarasso, a New York plastic surgeon, has said that queries about double chin reduction including liposuction and tucks increased during the Covid-19 quarantine in 2020. "Even an eight-year-old, if you bend their head down they're going to have extra fat," he said. (Haggin, 2020). Move around to prevent people from focusing on those features that are rendered unflattering by the camera. Ideally, you want to frame your head, neck and shoulders. People are drawn to faces. You want to be close enough to the screen to be "in their face" and yet not close enough to have a big nose. Blemish? Keep a little makeup handy.

Control the sound

Just like in a face-to-face presentation, you have to worry about sound. Do you have a good microphone? Some microphones sound hollow or even tinny. Sound quality is one part of a virtual presentation that is often overlooked. Do you know where the microphone on your computer is? I just looked for the one on my computer. I have no idea! If you are going to be moving around to get articles to demonstrate something or control pieces of equipment, you may want to invest in a clip-on microphone.

I am sure that when watching news or an interview on television you will have sometimes noticed a pause between when a speaker asks a question or makes a comment and when the reporter on the other line starts to talk or answer. This is caused by a sound transmission delay. Remember to pause after you ask a question or after someone finishes talking. It is best to remind your audience about this problem before you ask for any audience participation or questions. But don't you be afraid to talk over people to get their attention. Your meeting—you're the boss!

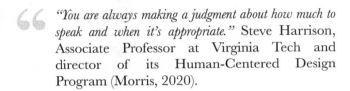

"You are always making a judgment about how much to speak and when it's appropriate." Steve Harrison, Associate Professor at Virginia Tech and director of its Human-Centered Design Program (Morris, 2020).

Control the lighting

Spend time really thinking and looking at how you look on screen. Are you well lit? The main light should be in front and slightly above you. If there is a window or doorway behind you, place something over it like a colored sheet to prevent any glare or hide a big black hallway—or find a different background. Natural lighting is usually best, but in your home or office that might not always be possible. My office used to be in a windowless basement! You may want to beg, borrow, or buy supplemental lighting, but you would be surprised by what you can do with the lamps you have around the house.

Photographers use a basic three light setup for portraits, cover shots, and whenever they want to highlight how a person looks. First there is the Key Light. This is the main light on the subject. It is usually places at a 45-degree angle to the camera. The Key Light is the brightest light and in portraiture is usually placed slightly above a model's eye level, angling downward. The second light is the Fill Light. It is in the same position as the Key Light but on the opposite side. It is less intense than the Key Light. The Fill Light's job is to fill in the shadows caused by the Key Light. The third light is the Back (or Rim or Hair or Shoulder) Light. The Back Light is placed opposite the Key Light and is pointed towards the back of the head. The Back Light frames the head and shoulders, gives depth to the subject, and a shiny glow to their hair.

OK, OK, this may sound like I'm going overboard! I am not. How the lighting falls on you and on your background helps with the overall ambience of your presentation or meeting. I do know two people who actually set up lighting like this in their homes: one male, one female; one in education, one in business. I do need to stress the importance of lighting though. Lighting, be it poor or proper, affects everything about how you and your surroundings look online.

Dress for success

No matter where you are actually presenting from, dress appropriately. Perhaps I should say dress professionally. Avoid contrasting colors and busy designs. Big flowers are out, along with stripes and plaids. Avoid wearing red or white or any color that is dominant in your background. Don't wear flashy jewelry or jewelry that may make noise or dangle and could distract your audience. Play to the camera. Again, make sure that you look directly at the camera when speaking.

Always try to look your best. You don't need a large wardrobe for your virtual meetings. Many people have a "zoom outfit" they usually wear. This may include a few different shirts and ties, tops, or necklaces.

Or perhaps not:

Joe Farrell, a vice president for the Funny or Die comedy group wore the same shirt (short-sleeve, button-down in black, red and white plaid) on video calls for 70 consecutive days (as a joke). "My ego thought someone would notice," he said. Even though he Zoomed six co-workers every day and up to 50 entertainment industry executives week after week, no one noticed. He finally started telling people what he was doing. "Every time I've outed myself, they say, 'Oh, yeah,' and they pull up two shirts hanging on the back of their chair." (Kat, 2020).

"Initially I would look in my closet for them (a turtleneck, a V-neck T-shirt and a jacket)," says Gretchen Young, a vice president at Hachette Book Group. "Then I said 'I'm hanging them on my bedroom door.' Then I just had them sitting on a chair in my dining room where I set up my desk." (Stein, 2020).

Many apparel companies now have special clothing targeted at the 'Zoom apparel market'. Suitsupply (http://suitsupply.com) even sells shirts for about $100 that only button half way down—appropriately just out of virtual camera range.

Be aware of your surroundings

Just as in a face-to-face presentation, your virtual audience judges you the instant your picture appears on the monitor. I set up a camera in our living room for security when we leave on a vacation. It shocked me to see what the room looked like. I never realized how messy it was. I am sorry to say that I vowed never to show a still or live shot from that camera to anyone! Take a look around where you will be presenting. You do not want any distractions on screen. We immediately think about pictures and wall hangings, but there are other potential distractions as well. Often the computer's camera is lower than your head. In this case, much of your ceiling may be visible. Last night I was watching a political interview on television. It was obvious that the person being interviewed was looking down at his computer. I swear that he had photos and awards on the ceiling behind him!

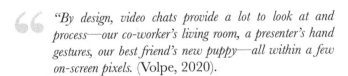

"By design, video chats provide a lot to look at and process—our co-worker's living room, a presenter's hand gestures, our best friend's new puppy—all within a few on-screen pixels. (Volpe, 2020).

What your audience sees on the monitor is important. The whole monitor! People will look at your room and use what they see to judge you. Is there a table or a bookshelf behind you with books on it? Check the titles and the topics very carefully. If they can read the titles, many will. Is the room a mess? Try not to have a window in the background. No matter what you try to do with it, it will be distracting. If the window is covered with a nice set of solid color drapes, you might be able to use this as your background. Just remember that you don't want loud or patterned prints. It is best to use a professional or virtual background that can be added by the computer as your background.

Many platforms, such as Zoom for instance, allow you to superimpose a background image behind you, kind of like the weatherperson on television. S/he is actually standing in front of a blank background—a 'green screen'—and a computer in the studio is generating the weather map you see behind the weatherperson on your television. The weatherperson is looking at a monitor off-screen to the left (or right) of the camera—at the same picture (and weather map background) you are seeing on your screen—and moving accordingly. It does take some practice! If you are going to superimpose a background, please don't put up a distracting one: no south-sea islands or zombies banging at the window. The Microsoft Teams platform has a neat feature. It allows you to blur your background.

If you are not speaking, make sure that you mute your sound. My computer is currently five feet away from a grand-father clock. This is a bad place to have an online meeting. It would be very distracting if the clock went off while I was in the middle of a live online meeting!

A week ago, I met up with several friends over Zoom. The sound of a friend's clock ticking from another room came through loud and clear. One of the other participants asked if someone was sitting on a time bomb! You don't want the kids to be talking in the background or the dog barking inside or outside of the house, or even a siren in the street outside.

> *"The new-economy employee has been working from home, where his biggest complaint may be an inability to conduct a Zoom call without a dog barking or child interrupting."* (Holmes, 2020).

Back in April of 2020, Google Meets came out with a really impressive AI background noise cancellation feature. You probably have seen demos or been at meetings where this is used. It actually cancels out sounds like dogs barking, children talking, clocks, and other background noise. The actually processing happens in the cloud, and because of this it is easier to port this feature to a wide variety of hardware. The noise-cancellation feature is on by default and can be toggled off from the audio menu in Google Meet's settings. Several other platforms have announced that they are working to incorporate a similar feature.

> *"My husband has a new quarantine hobby of Zoom bombing my conference calls. The colleagues I'm meeting with always see him before I do. It's so strange to see a team of people laughing while you're presenting and then realizing something ridiculous is going on behind you. Friends started mailing him Halloween costumes. Never a dull moment in this household!"* —Cara Fields of Greenfield, Indiana. (Thomason, 2020).

PoweredPointer 66: Be aware of your surroundings

Test the platform beforehand

It is best to be in position *at least* 30 minutes before your presentation to test and review the technology. Remember everything I said several chapters ago about knowing the room? Now I am saying: "Know the platform." How do you adjust the sound? How do you share your computer monitor on-screen? Split screens are nice, but small. Can you change that? This can be really important if you usually use a different platform. You don't want to hit the wrong button or fail to find the right one in the 'heat' of your performance!

PoweredPointer 67: Practice using the platform until you are really comfortable

Be prepared

Make sure that you have everything you need at your finger-tips. Lay everything out beforehand. You don't want to have to rustle through papers or objects to find what you want while you are speaking. This is a main reason to set up early.

Keep it simple

By this time you should know this phrase by heart. It is really important when your audience is peering at a small computer screen or a television monitor placed several feet away from them. Even if your information is projected onto a larger screen, it may be difficult for them to read. Rooms are usually not pitch dark, and the ambient light can make it even harder for your audience to see your slides, let alone read their text. Remember to use large, simple fonts with contrasting colors and avoid any of the animations and noises that are available in presentation programs. Most of these are highly distracting.

Stand up

Try this even though it may feel and sound odd. It is difficult to feel energized if you are alone with just your notes and your computer full of faces. After all, you can't hear or see a real audience. Audiences connect with energized presenters and become more interested and energized themselves as a result. How do you really connect and be energized with your audience in a virtual situation like this? One way is to do your presentation standing up. Standing up makes you fell like you are really presenting and actually increases your energy level. (Duarte, n.d.) You don't have to invest in one of those stand-up desks to make it work. Just place your computer on a high cardboard box on top of the desk. Remember what I said about doing what is comfortable for your audience and not to you? If you have to sit, make sure you avoid slouching or leaning back in your chair.

Monitor yourself with a mirror

If the platform you are using does not allow you to see yourself, you may want to set up a mirror to monitor how you look to your audience. This is also the case if you have to minimize yourself to get more audience members showing on the screen. Remember, since you will be spending much of your time looking at the camera, it is difficult to get feedback from your audience's body language or faces.

Enjoy yourself

Face-to-face presentations and meetings can be anxiety producing for the same reason that virtual presentations may be less stressful. It comes down to where the audience is located. Many of us have increased anxiety when we face a room full of people but have less anxiety when we are alone staring at a camera. Perhaps it is because we invite so many people into our living room through our television set on an almost daily basis that we are used to a full living room!

Look like you are enjoying yourself even if you are not!

If you are enjoying yourself, your audience will enjoy themselves more than if you look like you aren't. Your enjoyment and enthusiasm is infectious will get the audience going. Model the enthusiasm that you want to create! Research actually shows that happy people learn and retain more information than bored and disinterested people (Abbajay, 2020). You may not be able to use your whole body, but remember to use your face. Express yourself, smile, and animate your face!

No eating during a meeting

I was just on a FaceTime meeting. One of the participants was eating a very early lunch . It was really distracting. Please, no eating, snacking, or drinking. This should go without saying. If you are participating in a business meeting, don't be eating your breakfast or lunch during the meeting unless the moderator says it is OK. Even then you will notice that it is very distracting. If you are the moderator, please give your group fair warning that eating will not be tolerated. Participants can always catch a bite before a luncheon meeting.

Practice, practice, practice

A survey I read found that speakers spend more time preparing for offline presentations than virtual ones (AMA, 2019). Throughout this book I stressed that it is very important that you practice your presentation many, many times. Use the virtual platform and equipment just as you would if you were presenting in front of a 'real' group. Many platforms allow you to actually record yourself as you rehearse. When you practice, start at the very beginning and continue all the way through to the end. Remember to time your presentation as well. Since we really don't see ourselves the way others do, have a friend sit through one of your practice sessions to provide you with feedback. If you don't understand what your friend's feedback means, perhaps you could view a recording of your presentation together and go through their comments. It is important to have another pair of eyes review your presentation.

PoweredPointer 68: Practice with a friend

That is really about it. You should now be ready to have a powerful presentation or meeting in a face-to-face environment and in this new virtual world. As you just read, many of the things you learned about face-to-face presentations and meetings also apply to virtual presentations and meetings. The major differences are that you do have to remember to practice with your equipment until it is second nature and to find ways to hold your audience's attention.

CHAPTER 12

YOU ARE AT THE FINISH LINE

W ell, that is about it. You really have hit the finish line. Or perhaps you are now at the starting line! Now you just have to use everything you learned, produced, and gathered to make one final push over that line.

You are going to be a great success! You have taken on an important human task. You are helping, educating, or discussing important information relevant to your audience. You are passing on knowledge, accolades and/or wisdom to the little part of the world soon to be sitting in front of you. Who knows how many others you will be affecting. You have done everything you have to do. Let's take a look:

- You have accepted the invitation to present, give a speech, or give a keynote address. Or you may have answered a call for presentations and the powers that be thought that what you are going to speak about would fit right in. Anyway you look at it, they want you!

- You carried out an audience analysis. You have reviewed and checked the items in *PoweredGuide 1: Audience Analysis* to help you understand your audience. You know whom you will be talking to. You know their sex, age range, interests, something about their line of work, and even why they are in your audience. You know something about how they talk and what their knowledge level of the subject is. You even know something about how you should present to them and what you should avoid. And more importantly, you know you are ready for them!

- You wrote down your goal so you know where you want your presentation or talk to end up. You wrote down the steps or objectives you have to accomplish to achieve your goal. You wrote down the arguments you will use to build your steps one by one and lead you and your audience smoothly to the next step in the process. You also developed a great opening and a great conclusion for your presentation or talk. Your introduction will make the audience want to stay and listen to what you want to say, and your conclusion will tie up all of the pieces into one neat package.

- You put all the steps to your goal on a PowerPoint or on note cards if you are giving a speech. You have practiced what you are going to say and how you are going to say it. You also remember the peanut. You don't have to say the exact same thing for every bullet point every time you present. If you do this presentation several more times, you will most likely say slightly different words, but the essence of your presentation or speech will shine through. The essence of your talk is your PowerPoint bullets. You have reviewed and used *PoweredGuide 3: Planning Your Presentation* to help you with this task.

- If you find that you have extra time towards the end of your assigned time, you know what to do. You have supplemental information for the audience and/or starter questions if the audience has none, and you know how to keep control if they do have questions.

- You have practiced your facial expressions and gestures. You know that you will be able to hold your audience's attention. You may come up with more ideas as you go through your presentation or speech. It's going to be fun. It really is. Hey, you are an actor on a stage!

- You have got this. Yes, you may have the jitters as the time for your presentation or speech gets closer. This is not a Hallmark movie where someone is asked to talk about something out of the blue and dives right in totally unfazed. You have read enough to understand that a bit (or even a lot) of nerves is normal! Many presenters actually feel that nervousness makes them do a better presentation or speech. We all get those jitters. You know how to control the jitters and know what you are going to say and how you are going to say it. It may not be perfect and you may forget a point or two. This is not something to worry about. You can add the points as you remember them or add them when you are finished if necessary. The essence of your presentation is your PowerPoint, so that will have most of what you want to get across right on the screen. You will be adding information and perhaps entertainment. You've got this!

- You have a good idea about what will be available in your presentation room. You also know how to research the venue a bit when you arrive. You have looked over and filled out *PoweredGuide 2: Know the Room* so you have a good idea of what to expect when you get there. You know what to look for and what you will need to find during this room inspection. You also know what to ask about the room well before you arrive at the venue.

PoweredGuide 5: Arrival Checklist helped you with this.

- You know what you need to do to set up the room for your presentation, such as where to put the water and small candies. You have retrieved what you will need and have everything in your prep bag. *PoweredGuide 4: Your Prep Bag* helped you fill your prep bag.

- If you have a chance, you will go out and talk with your audience before your performance. *PoweredGuide 7: Meeting the Audience* will help you with some of the questions you should ask them or talk with them about.

- You have filled out *PoweredGuide 6: Who am I?* You will use this to look at before the presentation or to give to the room monitor or person who will be introducing you. If you are not introducing yourself, don't forget to tell the person who will be introducing you how to pronounce your name if necessary!

- Before the room monitor or you introduce yourself, you know how to focus on relaxing, and you will try to take a few deep breaths. You know that at this point even the most seasoned presenter or speaker is nervous. But you know what you are going to say and how you are going to say it. You have rehearsed your presentation or speech and know that you are ready to take charge!

- Now, put on a smile and dig right in. You will be fabulous. If you forget a few things, don't worry, your PowerPoint is your presentation. You can always add important details later.

- Don't forget to review how your presentation went, what you did well, and what you wish you had done differently. *PoweredGuide 10: Time to Review Your Presentation* should be a big help with this review.

Presenting is like riding a bike or playing tennis, or bird watching. You get better the more you practice. You never can tell when you may be called upon to participate in a face-to-face or virtual meeting or conference. This could be work related, neighborhood related or perhaps even hobby related. Be prepared. There are plenty of opportunities for you to be a part of a presentation or discussion group. The more you become involved, the more comfortable you will become. And… you will probably enjoy doing it!

 "A book may give you excellent suggestions on how best to conduct yourself in the water, but sooner or later you must get wet …" Dale Carnegie (2009).

REFERENCES CITED

Chapter 2

Cannon, L. (2000). *President Reagan: The role of a lifetime.* Boston, MA: PublicAffairs.

Lee, C. (2006). Role of a movie director? [online] Yahoo Answers. Available at http://answers.yahoo.com/question/index?qid=20061210110724AAmERnm

CreativeMMS. (2012). Wdw: Web designs we love:sanebox. [online] Creative MMS Blog 29 February. Available at: http://www.creativemms.com/wdw-web-designs-we-love-sanebox/

Ellet, J. (2010). How long does it take your customer to form an opinion? [online] nFusion. Available at: http://nfusion.com/blog/how-long-does-it-take-your-customer-to-form-an-opinion/

Empire Magazine. (2020). Film studies 101: Who does what on a movie set? [online] Available at: https://www.empireonline.com/movies/features/film-studies-101-movie/

Medium. (2015). Learning from a world-class designer and typographer, Erik Spiekermann. [online]. Available at: https://medium.com/@Reedsy/learning-from-a-world-class-designer-and-typographer-erik-spiekermann-1801eac729ac

Chapter 3

Adams, S. (2013). Your voice could cost you hundreds of thousands of dollars, study shows. *Forbes*. [online] Available at: http://www.forbes.com/sites/susanadams/2013/04/18/your-voice-could-be-costing-you-hundreds-of-thousands-of-dollars-study-shows/?utm_campaign=techtwittersf&utm_source=twitter&utm_medium=social

Argyle, M., Alkema, F. and Gilmour, R. (1971). The communication of friendly and hostile attitudes by verbal and non-verbal signals. *European Journal of Social Psychology*. 1(3): 385–402.

Braithwaite, L. (2007). The truth about 7% – 38% – 55%. [online] Speak Schmeak: Things I'm thinking about speakers and speaking. Available at: http://www.speakschmeak.com/2007/08/truth-about-7-38-55.html

Chang, C. (2013). Men with deeper voices are more successful. *ENT* blog. [online] Available at: http://fauquierent.blogspot.com/2013/04/men-with-deeper-voices-are-more.html

Devito, J.A. (1999). *Messages: Building interpersonal communication skills*. 4th ed. New York: Addison-Wesley, p.37.

Doyno, S. (2013). Dress for success? Tips for your job interview style. *Yahoo News*. [online] Available at: http://news.yahoo.com/blogs/katies-take-abc-news/dressed-success-tips-job-interview-style-175736455.html?vp=1

Dunbar, P. (2011). How Laurence Olivier gave Margaret the voice that went down in history. *The Daily Mail*. [online] Available at: http://www.dailymail.co.uk/news/article-2055214/How-Laurence-Olivier-gave-Margaret-Thatcher-voice-went-history.html

Fasbinder, F. (2017). Use these 3 vocal techniques to command the room like Margaret Thatcher and Obama. *Inc.* [online]. Available at: https://www.inc.com/fia-fasbinder/science-shows-people-respond-to-stronger-deeper-voices-how-to-train-your-voice-like-margaret-thatcher-obama.html

Goleman, D. (2005). *Emotional intelligence.* 10th ed. New York: Bantam Books, p.20

Goman, C. K. (2011). Seven seconds to make a first impression. *Forbes.* [online] Available at: http://www.forbes.com/sites/carolkinseygoman/2011/02/13/seven-seconds-to-make-a-first-impression/

Hyatt, M. (n.d.). How to build (or rebuild) trust. [online] Michael Hyatt: Helping Leaders Leverage Influence. Available at:: http://michaelhyatt.com/how-to-build-trust.html

Iveson, M. (2012). Ten silent super-stars facing the advent of 'talkies'. [online] Shadowlocked: Find the Future. Available at: http://www.shadowlocked.com/201203072430/lists/10-silent-super-stars-facing-the-advent-of-talkies.html

Khazan, O. (2016). Would you really like Hillary more is she sounded different? *The Atlantic.* [online]. Available at: https://www.theatlantic.com/science/archive/2016/08/hillarys-voice/493565/

Marean, P. (2009). The importance of voice. *Cape Cod Times.* [online] Available at: http://www.capecodonline.com/apps/pbcs.dll/article?AID=/20090529/LIFE/905290301

Gentlemen prefer blondes – diamonds are a girl's best friend. (2018). [YouTube video] Marilyn Monroe Video Archives. [online] Available at: https://www.youtube.com/watch?v=bfsnebJd-BI

Mehrabian, A. (1971). *Nonverbal communication.* Marceline, MO: Wadsworth Publishing Co.

Mehrabian, A. (1980). *Silent Messages: Implicit communication of emotion and attitudes.* 2nd ed.. Marceline, MO: Wadsworth Publishing Co.

Mitchell, O. (n.d.). Mehrabian and nonverbal communication. [online] Speaking about presenting. Available at: http://www.speakingaboutpresenting.com/presentation-myths/mehrabian-nonverbal-communication-research/

Mouland, B. (2010). The husky voice of seduction: A lower tone when speaking to the opposite sex is a 'sure sign of attraction'. *Daily Mail.* [online] Available at: http://www.dailymail.co.uk/sciencetech/article-1268626/The-husky-voice-seduction-A-lower-tone-speaking-opposite-sex-sure-sign-attraction.html

Sarkis, S.A. (2011). 43 quotes on body language. *Psychology Today*. [online] Available at: https://www.psychologytoday.com/us/blog/here-there-and-everywhere/201109/43-quotes-body-language

Smith, E. R., and Mackie, D. M. (2007). *Social psychology.* 3rd ed. New York: Psychology Press, Taylor & Francis Group, pp. 57, 86).

Strong, W. F., and Cook, J. A. (2005). *Persuasion: Strategies for speakers.* 2nd ed. Dubuque, IA: Kendall/Hunt Publishing Co., pp. 38—39.

Twain, M. (n.d.) Mark Twain quotes. [online] Brainyquote. Available at: https://www.brainyquote.com/citation/quotes/mark_twain_124428

Willis, J., and Todorov, A. (2006). First impressions: Making up your mind after 100 ms exposure to a face. *Psychological Science*, 17:592-598.

Chapter 4

Kettenhofen, C. (2006). Presentation skills: knowing your audience. [online] Ezine. Available at: http://ezinearticles.com/expert/Colleen_Kettenhofen/38379

Chapter 5

American College Health Association. (2019). Instructions for writing learning objectives and content. [online] Available at: https://www.acha.org/AnnualMeeting19/AnnualMeeting19/Writing_Objectives.aspx

Chapter 6

Drucker, P. F. (1954). *The practice of management.* New York: Harper Business.

Enderle, R. (2020). Microsoft just fixed powerpoint: you're

going to love presenter coach. Available at: https://www.
computerworld.com/article/3537609/microsoft-just-fixed-
powerpoint-youre-going-to-love-presenter-coach.html

Federal Trade Commission (FTC). (2017). FTC releases
annual summary of consumer complaints. [online] Available
at: https://www.ftc.gov/news-events/press-releases/2017/
03/ftc-releases-annual-summary-consumer-complaints

Chapter 7

Abbajay, M. (2020). Best practices for virtual presentations: 15
expert tips that work for everyone. *Forbes* [online] Available at
https://www.forbes.com/sites/maryabbajay/2020/04/20/
best-practices-for-virtual-presentations-15-expert-tips-that-
work-for-everyone/#44cf5e033d19

Enoch, N. (2014). Mein camp: Unseen pictures of Hitler…in
a very tight pair of lederhosen. *The Daily Mail.* [online] Available at: https://www.dailymail.co.uk/news/article-2098223/
Pictures-Hitler-rehearsing-hate-filled-speeches.html

Hitler, A., Murphy, J. & Carruthers, B. (2011). *Mein kampf: the
official 1939 edition.* London: Archive Media Publishing Ltd.

McLellan, D. (2020). How to give a presentation like a pro.
[online] Entrepreneur.com. Available at: https://www.
entrepreneur.com/article/346399

Hitler's speech rehearsal visualized. (n.d.). [YouTube video] Moorhouse, R. [online] Available at: https://www.youtube.com/
watch?v=XnKaYcLB6w0&bpctr=1542382385

Philip, C. (2019). Adolf Hitler practiced his body language –
assessing Hitler's bizarre gestures and postures. [online] Body
language project. Available at: http://bodylanguageproject.
com/articles/adolf-hitler-practised-his-body-language-
assessing-hitlers-bizarre-gestures-and-postures/

Chapter 8

Miller, F. (2016). Three things not to do when answering questions. [online] No sweat public speaking. Available at: from

https://nosweatpublicspeaking.com/three-things-not-to-do-when-answering-questions/

Skills You Need. (2020). Dealing with presentation questions. [online] Available at: https://www.skillsyouneed.com/present/presentation-questions.html

Chapter 9

AZ Quotes. (n.d.). AZ quotes authors – s. [online] Available at https://www.azquotes.com/quote/214266

BrainyQuotes (n.d.). Stage fright quotes. [online] Brainy Quotes. Available at: https://www.brainyquote.com/topics/stage_fright

Carter, J. (2018). Can we ever get over stage fright and performing anxiety? *Psychology Today.* [online] Available at: https://www.psychologytoday.com/us/blog/stress-is-laughing-matter/201805/can-we-ever-get-over-stage-fright-and-performing-anxiety

Croston, G. (2012). The things we fear more than death. *Psychology Today.* [online] Available at: https://www.psychologytoday.com/blog/the-real-story-risk/201211/the-thing-we-fear-more-death

Dwyer, K.K. & Davidson, M.M. (2012). Is public speaking really more feared than death? [online] Available at: http://www.tandfonline.com/doi/full/10.1080/08824096.2012.667772

Frisbee, E. (2019). Dry mouth: causes, symptoms, and treatment. [online] WebMD. Available at: https://www.webmd.com/oral-health/ss/slideshow-dry-mouth

Garber, R.I. (2012). Either way you look at it, public speaking really is not our greatest fear. [online] Joyful public speaking. Available at: http://joyfulpublicspeaking.blogspot.com/2012/10/either-way-you-look-at-it-public_23.html

Harvard Health. (2016). Relaxation techniques: breath control helps quell errant stress response. *Harvard Health Publishing.* [online] Available at: https://www.health.harvard.

edu/mind-and-mood/relaxation-techniques-breath-control-helps-quell-errant-stress-response

Hickson, A. (2016). One thing these 10 faves have in common. [online] Refinery 29. Available at: https://www.refinery29.com/en-us/2016/05/111114/celebrity-quotes-stage-fright-anxiety

Kettenhofen, C. (2006). Presentation skills: knowing your audience. [online] Ezine. Available at: http://ezinearticles.com/expert/Colleen_Kettenhofen/38379

Microsoft (2019). Say hello to presenter coach, powerpoint's new ai-powered tool that will help you nail your next presentation. Available at: https://news.microsoft.com/europe/2019/06/18/say-hello-to-presenter-coach-powerpoints-new-ai-powered-tool-which-will-help-you-nail-your-next-presentation/

Newlyn, E. (2019). January intentions: balancing physical fitness with mental fitness. [online] Yoga matters. Available at: https://www.yogamatters.com/blog/january-intentions-balancing-physical-fitness-with-mental-fitness/

Salinas, T.J. (2017). Dry mouth treatment: tips for controlling dry mouth. [online] The Mayo Clinic. Available at: https://www.mayoclinic.org/diseases-conditions/dry-mouth/expert-answers/dry-mouth/FAQ-20058424

ThinkExist.com. (2012). Jerry Seinfeld quotes. [online] Available at: http://thinkexist.com/quotes/jerry_seinfeld/ [Video also available: on YouTube: https://www.youtube.com/watch?v=kL7fTLjFzAg].

Thorpe, J.R. (2014). Nine quotes about public speaking fear and technique to help inspire you. [online] Bustle. Available at: https://www.bustle.com/articles/49958-9-quotes-about-public-speaking-fear-and-technique-to-help-inspire-you

Wilkinson, A. (n.d.). Natural remedies for dry mouth that will make you feel so much better. *Reader's Digest*. [online] Available at: https://www.rd.com/health/wellness/natural-remedies-dry-mouth/

Chapter 10

Carnegie, D. (2009). *How to win friends and influence people – reissue edition.* New York: Simon & Schuster.

Gottsman, D (2012). Business etiquette: how to introduce a presenter. [online] Public words. Available at: http://www.publicwords.com/2011/11/26/how-to-introduce-a-speaker-the-art-of-giving-and-receiving-a-great-introduction/

Kettenhofen, C. (2006). Presentation skills: knowing your audience. [online] Ezine. Available at: http://ezinearticles.com/expert/Colleen_Kettenhofen/38379

Marshall, L.B. (2017). What to say when introducing a speaker. [online] Quick and dirty tips. Available at: http://www.quickanddirtytips.com/business-career/public-speaking/what-to-say-when-introducing-a-speaker

Morgan, N. (2011). How to introduce a speaker – the art of giving (and receiving) a great introduction. [online] Public words. Available at: http://www.publicwords.com/2011/11/26/how-to-introduce-a-speaker-the-art-of-giving-and-receiving-a-great-introduction/

Nastasi, A. (2014). 100 famous directors' rules of filmmaking. *Flavorwire.* [online] Available at: https://www.flavorwire.com/465913/100-famous-directors-rules-of-filmmaking

Chapter 11

Abbajay, M. (2020). Best practices for virtual presentations: 15 expert tips that work for everyone. *Forbes* [online] Available at: https://www.forbes.com/sites/maryabbajay/2020/04/20/best-practices-for-virtual-presentations-15-expert-tips-that-work-for-everyone/#44cf5e033d19

AMA. (2019). Perfect your virtual presentations. [online] Available at https://www.amanet.org/articles/perfect-your-virtual-presentations/

Duarte, M. (n.d.). Virtual presentation tips. [online] Available at: https://www.duarte.com/virtual-presentation-tips/

Feldman, B. (2020). Is it safe to use zoom? *New Yorker Magazine* [online] Available at: https://nymag.com/intelligencer/2020/04/the-zoom-app-has-a-lot-of-security-problems.html

Haggin, P. (2020). Next videoconferencing test – webcams add 10 pounds under the jawline; raising the camera and taping back skin. *The Wall Street Journal* [online] Available at: https://www.wsj.com/articles/virus-videoconferencing-hiding-your-on-screen-double-chin-11590069979?mod=tech_lead_pos13

Hansen, J. (2020). How to keep your audience engaged in an online presentation. *Visme blog* [online] Available: at https://visme.co/blog/engage-audience-online-presentation/

Holmes, J. (2020). The covid political earthquake. [online] Available at: https://www.wsj.com/articles/the-covid-political-earthquake-11590706829?mod=searchresults&page=1&pos=1

Kat. (2020). What's your zoom shirt"? Corporette. [online] Available at: https://corporette.com/zoom-shirt-for-women/

Morris, B. (2020). Why does Zoom exhaust you? Science has an answer. *The Wall Street Journal* [online] Available at: https://www.wsj.com/articles/why-does-zoom-exhaust-you-science-has-an-answer-11590600269?mod=searchresults&page=1&pos=12

Phuse. (n.d.). 8 tips to improve virtual presentations. [online] Available at: https://www.phuse.eu/blog/8-tips-to-improve-virtual-presentations-new-

Stein, J. (2020). The video call is starting. Time to put on your Zoom shirt. *The New York Times.* [online] Available at: https://www.nytimes.com/2020/06/29/business/zoom-shirt.html

Thomason, A. (2020). Husband dresses in costumes to embarrass his wife during her Zoom meetings. *The Western Journal.* [online] Available at: https://www.westernjournal.com/husband-dresses-costumes-embarrass-wife-zoom-meetings/

TrustRadius. (2020). Web and videoconferencing software. *TrustRadius.* [online] Available at: https://www.trustradius.com/web-conferencing?f=0#products

Uose, H.T. (2020). The trauma of Zoom. *Medium.* [online] Available at: https://medium.com/@Hanna.Thomas/the-trauma-of-zoom-bb3609aa41b2

Volpe, A. (2020). Why you can't stop looking at your face on Zoom. *Elemental.* [online] Available at https://elemental. medium.com/why-you-cant-stop-looking-at-your-face-on-zoom-3391220ed1f9

OTHER USEFUL WEBSITES

Planning your presentation

Bell, M., Hunter, L., & O'Bryan, H. (n.d.). Planning for your oral presentation. [online] Available at: http://stemdiv.ucsc.e-du/files/4513/1717/0253/OralPresentationHO_2007.pdf
Columbia College. (2019). Giving presentations. [online] Available at: https://columbiacollege-ca.libguides.com/pre-sentations/planning
Mindtools. (n.d.). The presentation planner checklist. [online] Available at: https://www.mindtools.com/CommSkll/Presen-tationPlanningChecklist.htm
University of Leicester. (n.d.). Planning an effective presenta-tion. [online] Available at: https://www2.le.ac.uk/of-fices/ld/resources/presentations/planning-presentation

Rehearsing your presentation

Dlugen, A. (2008). Speech preparation #8: how to practice your presentation. [online] Available at: http://sixminutes.d-lugan.com/speech-preparation-8-practice-presentation/
Gallo, C. (n.d.). 5 key steps to rehearsing a presentation like the best ted speakers. [online] Available at: https://www.inc.-

com/carmine-gallo/5-key-steps-to-rehearsing-a-presentation-like-best-ted-speakers.html

Morgan, N. (n.d.). Seven ways to rehearse a speech. [online] Available at: https://publicwords.com/2012/07/26/seven-ways-to-rehearse-a-speech/

Schwertly, S. (2014). The complete guide to practicing before a presentation. [online] Available at: https://www.ethos3.com/2014/07/the-complete-guide-to-practicing-before-a-presentation/

Universal Class. (2020). Ways to rehearse your speech for an effective presentation. [online] Available at: https://www.universalclass.com/articles/business/rehearsing-your-speech-for-an-effective-presentation.htm

Audience analysis

DeCaro, P., Adams, T., & Jefferis, B. (n.d.). Audience analysis. [online] Available at: http://publicspeakingproject.org/PDF%20Files/aud%20analy%20web%201.pdf

Legault, N. (2011). 20+ questions to include in an audience analysis. [online] Available at: https://nlegault.ca/2011/11/28/20-questions-to-conduct-an-audience-analysis/

Thompson, S. (2017). How to analyze your audience before a presentation. [online] Available at: https://virtualspeech.com/blog/audience-analysis-speech

Thoughtline. (2019). Public speaking: 10 questions to analyze your audience. [online] Available at: https://www.throughlinegroup.com/2017/06/13/public-speaking-10-questions-to-analyze-your-audience/

University of Hawaii. (2002). Analyzing your audience. [online] Available at: https://www.hawaii.edu/mauispeech/html/analyzing_your_audience.html

Controlling anxiety

Cuncic, A. (2020). Tips for managing public speaking anxiety. [online] Available at: https://www.verywellmind.com/tips-for-managing-public-speaking-anxiety-3024336

Kim, L. (2014). 15 ways to calm your nerves before a big presentation. [online] Available at: https://www.inc.-com/larry-kim/15-power-up-tips-to-make-you-a-better-presenter.html

Sawchuk, C. (2017) How can I overcome my fear of public speaking? [online] Available at: https://www.mayoclinic.org/diseases-conditions/specific-phobias/expert-answers/fear-of-public-speaking/faq-20058416

University of Iowa. (n.d.). 30 ways to manage speaking anxiety. [online] Available at: https://counseling.uiowa.edu/self-help/30-ways-to-manage-speaking-anxiety/

PowerPoint design

Creative Research Presentations. (2019). 6 reasons you need good visuals in your presentation. [online] Available at: https://www.echorivera.com/blog/6reasonsvisuals

Dlugan, A. (2018). Slide charts: 20 guidelines for great presentation design. [online] Available at: http://sixminutes.dlugan.com/slide-charts/

Malhotra, A. (2016). 11 dos and don'ts of using image in presentations. [online] Available at: https://www.slideteam.net/blog/using-images-in-presentations-11-dos-and-donts

Stec, C. (2019). 21 great examples of powerpoint presentation design [+ templates]. [online] Available at: https://blog.hubspot.com/blog/tabid/6307/bid/6012/17-examples-of-great-presentation-design.aspx

Teten, D. (2013) How to add powerful (and legal) images to your presentation. *Forbes.* [online]. Available at: https://www.forbes.com/sites/davidteten/2013/08/15/how-to-add-powerful-and-legal-images-to-your-presentations/#19028cb46dea

The Total Communicator. (n.d.). Design your visuals for

maximum impact. [online] Available at: http://totalcommu-nicator.com/vol3_1/visuals.html

Trounce, D. (2019). 10 ways to make your PowerPoint slideshow more engaging. [online] Available at: https://helpdeskgeek.com/office-tips/10-ways-to-make-your-powerpoint-slideshow-more-engaging/

Improving presentation skills

Capes, A. (2020). Giving effective presentations: 5 ways to present your points with power, not just PowerPoint. [online] Available at: https://thinkscience.co.jp/en/articles/effective-presentations

Kessler, S. (n.d.). How to improve your presentation skills. [online] Available at: https://www.inc.com/guides/how-to-improve-your-presentation-skills.html

Kim, l. (2014). 20 ways to improve your presentation skills. [online] Available at: https://www.wordstream.-com/blog/ws/2014/11/19/how-to-improve-presentation-skills

Online presentation skills

Business.com. (2020). 7 powerful tips for highly productive online meetings. [online] Available at: https://www.business.-com/articles/7-powerful-tips-for-highly-productive-online-meetings/

deBara, D. (2020). The ultimate guide to remote meetings in 2020. *Slack.* [online] Available at https://slackhq.com/ulti-mate-guide-remote-meetings

Daum, K. (2014). 10 tips for giving great online presentations. *Inc.* [online] Available at: https://www.forbes.-com/sites/michellegreenwald/2020/03/30/9-secrets-to-great-online-presenting-in-corporations-and-academia/#556ad99d1a3f

Frisch, B. & Greene, C. (2020). What it takes to run a great virtual meeting. *Harvard Business Review.* [online] Available at:

https://hbr.org/2020/03/what-it-takes-to-run-a-great-virtual-meeting

Greenwald. M. (2020) 11 secrets to great interactive online presentations in companies and universities. *Forbes.* [online] Available at: https://www.forbes.com/sites/michellegreenwald/2020/03/30/9-secrets-to-great-online-presenting-incorporations-and-academia/#556ad99d1a3f

Thomas, F. (2020). 5 tips for conduction a virtual meeting. *Inc.* [online] Available at: https://www.inc.com/guides/2010/12/5-tips-for-conducting-a-virtual-meeting.html

#PowerPoint. (2018). How to present a PowerPoint presentation online? *Microsoft.* [online] Available at https://www.youtube.com/watch?v=Zpn_lyCKsv4

Misc.

Barnard, D. (2017). What are the benefits of public speaking? [online] Available at: https://virtualspeech.com/blog/what-are-the-benefits-of-public-speaking

Columbia College. (2019). Giving presentations. [online] Available at: https://columbiacollege-ca.libguides.com/presentations/planning

Ribus. (n.d.). Why public speaking matters today. [online] Available at: https://press.rebus.community/uwmpublicspeaking/chapter/why-is-public-speaking-important/

Spencer, L. (2018). What is public speaking? & why is it important? [online] Available at: https://business.tutsplus.com/tutorials/what-is-public-speaking--cms-31255

University of Hawaii. (2002). Speakers' advice to speakers. [online]. Available at: https://www.hawaii.edu/mauispeech/html/speaking_tips.htmlUniversity of Leicester. (n.d.). Planning an effective presentation. [online] Available at: https://www2.le.ac.uk/offices/ld/resources/presentations/planning-presentation

APPENDIX I

COMPLETE LIST OF POWEREDPOINTERS

1. Forget everything you ever been taught, read, heard or learned about presenting
2. Don't be yourself
3. Play to your audience
4. Audience members make up their minds about you virtually as soon as they see you
5. They have to trust you to believe you
6. First impressions are lasting impressions
7. Body language and your look − 55%
8. Dress one step above your audience
9. You must sound the part
10. Practice your bums!
11. Your words are important
12. Practice, practice, practice your timing and delivery
13. Properly placed pauses enhance your presentation
14. Humor can help your audience connect to you and your message
15. Know your audience
16. Know the room

17. Customize, customize, customize!
18. Give them a reason to pay attention
19. Your presentation should be concrete and sequential
20. Write down your goal and one to three objectives
21. Jumpstart your presentation with a real attention grabber
22. Your conclusion should be just the beginning for your audience
23. Think of your presentation as a peanut
24. Your bullets are your presentation
25. Keep it simple
26. Incorporate the lettering, color and quotation design points
27. Remember the visual design points
28. You are an actor on a stage.
29. You are the medium
30. The room is your stage
31. Keep it light
32. Control attention
33. Use the stronger areas of the stage
34. Try to keep the screen off to the side
35. Talk only to people, not your notes or the screen
36. Work the whole room
37. Don't scan the room. Lock on to people's eyes for three to five seconds
38. Use your voice to energize both your presentation and your audience
39. Use strong gestures to emphasize points and to 'paint images'
40. Don't make unnecessary movements
41. Avoid putting your hands together
42. Avoid 'toys', pointers, pocket change, jewelry, etc.
43. Do what works for the audience
44. Indicate in the introduction that you would like the audience to hold their questions until the end of the presentation

45. Ask if there are any questions with a raised hand
46. Point to the questioner with an open hand
47. Avoid using names unless you know everyone in the room
48. After the question is asked, break visual contact with the questioner and repeat or rephrase the question to the audience
49. Do not preface your answer
50. Employ the 25% – 75% eye contact rule
51. Prepare for questions ahead of time
52. People would rather be dead than speak in public
53. Organize your material
54. Visualize your presentation
55. Practice, practice, practice
56. Deep breaths before you go on will help you relax
57. Focus on relaxing
58. Release tension with isometric exercises
59. Get to know the audience
60. Maintain eye contact with your audience
61. Reduce or cut out coffee consumption
62. Reduce foods that contain cholesterol and fat
63. Preparation will reduce stress and greatly enhance presentation success
64. You are well prepared and will do just fine!
65. Holding your audience's attention is your number one goal
66. Be aware of your surroundings
67. Practice using the platform until you are really comfortable
68. Practice with a friend

APPENDIX II

POWEREDGUIDES

1. Audience Analysis
2. Know the Room
3. Planning Your Presentation
4. Your Prep Bag
5. Arrival Checklist
6. Who am I?
7. Meeting the Audience
8. Reducing Anxiety Checklist
9. Rehearsal Checklist and Comments
10. Time to Review Your Presentation
11. Virtual Presentation or Meeting Prep Sheet

POWEREDGUIDE 1:
AUDIENCE ANALYSIS

How many people will be attending the function?

Attending your presentation?

Audience affiliation or company:

Your goal:

Who will be attending the presentation? (If more than one group, use percentages. Additional comments for each one can be written on the right.)
- ☐ End users
- ☐ Trainers
- ☐ Students
- ☐ Administrators
- ☐ Other:

What business are they in?
- ☐ Education:
- ☐ Finance:
- ☐ Government:
- ☐ Service:
- ☐ Other:

How far up the chain of command are they?

What is the level of expertise of the audience?
(0 being no knowledge of the subject)
0 - 1 - 2 - 3 - 4 - 5 - 6 - 7 - 8 - 9 - 10

What is their level of education?
☐ K-12
☐ Technical SchoolBA/BS
☐ Masters/Terminal degree

Why are they attending the presentation?
☐ Interested in subject
☐ For more information
☐ Mandatory
☐ Licensing/CEU/Other requirement
☐ Other reasons for attending presentation:

Approximate age range:

Sex:
☐ Male   ☐ Female   ☐ Unknown

Religion (if relevant):
Race:
☐ Black
☐ Hispanic
☐ White
☐ Unknown
Ethnicity:

What will they be wearing?

How much do the audience members know about the subject?
(0 is no knowledge)
0 - 1 - 2 - 3 - 4 - 5 - 6 - 7 - 8 - 9 - 10

How interested will your audience be to be at your presentation?

(0 is not interested)

0 - 1 - 2 - 3 - 4 - 5 - 6 - 7 - 8 - 9 - 10

How relevant is the presentation topic to them?

(0 is not relevant)

0 - 1 - 2 - 3 - 4 - 5 - 6 - 7 - 8 - 9 - 10

Does the audience view your topic favorably, unfavorably, or neutrally?

□ F □ U □ N

Explain:

What do they already know about the topic of your presentation?

How enthusiastic will your audience be about being at your presentation?

(0 is not enthusiastic about being there)

0 - 1 - 2 - 3 - 4 - 5 - 6 - 7 - 8 - 9 - 10

What do you think the attention span of the audience will be?

Does the audience have any preconceived notions about the topic?

□ Y □ N

List:

Are any of these preconceived notions, misconceptions, or gaps in their knowledge that you must address?

What objections do you think the audience will have to the subject of your presentation?

Do you foresee any objections that you think the audience may have to you or someone like you presenting to them?

What relevant worldviews/values do the audience members have? i.e., what do they stand for and against? Like, dislike, political, religious, etc.

How does their worldview/values differ from yours?

What basic values do the audience members hold?

How do you hope to help the audience members?

What is in it for them?

What percent of the audience will understand the jargon? (Specialized language/terminology/'lingo' that members outside the group will not understand.)

What does the audience expect from you?

POWEREDGUIDE 2: KNOW THE ROOM

How many people are expected at your presentation?

What will the audience be seated on?
- ☐ Chairs
- ☐ Desks
- ☐ Other (explain):

How will the seats be arranged?

Will there be a podium?
☐ Yes ☐ No
Are you expected to use the podium?
☐ Yes ☐ No
Will there be a microphone?
☐ Yes ☐ No
Will you be expected to use it?
☐ Yes ☐ No

Will the microphone be:

- ☐ Stationary
- ☐ Handheld
- ☐ Clip-on (Lavalier)

What controls are there for outside light (window light)?
- ☐ Blinds
- ☐ Drapes
- ☐ Other (explain):
- ☐ No/poor control for outside light
- ☐ No outside light control needed

Will there be any outside noise or distractions? (If yes, how can you control this?)
- ☐ Yes ☐ No

What time of day will you present?

Will your presentation be before, during, or after lunch, breaks, and/or conference highlights?
- ☐ Yes ☐ No

What are the conference highlights concurrent with your presentation?

Are light switches readily available?
- ☐ Yes ☐ No
- If Yes, Location(s):
- If "Yes", are they on dimmers?
- If no, how will the room lighting be controlled?

Are electrical outlets readily available?
- ☐ Yes ☐ No
- If Yes, Location(s):

How will you get the power you need? (Will the venue supply extension cords?)

What types of AV equipment will be supplied?
- ☐ Extension cords
- ☐ Computer
- ☐ Projection equipment.

☐ Can you use your own computer?

☐ Do you have the proper adapters for the projection equipment?

Will someone be available to help you set up your presentation?

☐ Yes ☐ No

(If No, where can you find help?)

Will someone be in the room before the presentation?

☐ Yes ☐ No

Will this person be available to:

☐ Help with seating

☐ Hand out evaluations

☐ Introduce you if necessary?

☐ In the room during the presentation?

☐ Will this person keep time?

☐ In the room after the presentation?

☐ Collect evaluations.

☐ Hand out materials.

How do you get your presentation materials/equipment into the building and keep it safe?

How close is the parking and/or unloading area?

Will there be someone available to help you if necessary?

Where can you safely store your presentation materials/equipment before and after my presentation?

POWEREDGUIDE 3:
PLANNING YOUR
PRESENTATION

What is the topic of your presentation?

How much time will you have to present?

What physical constraints does the room have?

What is the GOAL of your presentation? (The verb in a goal is not measurable.)

List your objectives. (You should have one objective for each half hour of presentation time, and each objective should contain a measurable verb.)
What are your arguments for each of your objectives?
(Continue on the back if necessary.)
Objective One:
Objective Two:
Objective Three:

How will you tie your objectives together?
Objective One to Objective Two:
Objective Two to Objective Three:

How will you introduce your presentation?

How will you conclude your presentation so as to pull everything together?

How do you want the audience to leave your presentation?
- ☐ With a call to action.
- ☐ With specific knowledge on the subject.
- ☐ Other:

Are you going to have handouts, and if so, what kind?

What AV equipment will you need?

POWEREDGUIDE 4: YOUR PREP BAG

Checklist:

☐ Tic-Tacs or other very small candy.

☐ Water bottles or containers.

☐ Computer containing your presentation.

☐ Presentation.

☐ Presentation backup copy (ies)—thumb drives.

☐ Paper copy of your presentation to review before you present and to take notes on after your presentation.

☐ Paper copy of your presentation and handouts and/or URL where handouts are posted.

☐ Business cards. Available online for as little as $10 per 100.

☐ Travel clock.

☐ Notepad. To collect names, comments, etc.

☐ Pens/pencils.

☐ Extra computer wires, extension cord, connectors, adapters, plugs.

☐ Extra batteries, charger.

☐ Snacks: granola bars, etc.

☐ Note cards.

POWEREDGUIDE 5: ARRIVAL CHECKLIST

☐ You have arrived at the venue early.

☐ You have double-checked to make sure that you have brought everything from home. (Prep Bag, computer, presentation, handouts, etc.)

What have you forgotten that you will need to get before you present?

☐ You have received presenter's information from the venue/organization.

Questions that you want to be sure to ask:
    What is the presentation room number?
    Where is the room located?
    When is the room going to be available for me to set up?

☐ You have found the speaker's room.

What equipment and services are available?

How do you contact someone from the speaker's room during your presentation?

☐ You have found the equipment room.

Will the equipment be in your presentation room early?
　　☐ Yes ☐ No

☐ You know how to get technical help if required.
　　Name(s) you need to know:
　　Phone numbers or extensions:

You know where to get technical help if required.
　　☐ Yes ☐ No
　　Location:

Do you have to use a microphone?
　　☐ Yes ☐ No
　　Is it attached in place or is it clip-on (Lavalier)?
　　☐ Yes ☐ No
　　Will someone help set you up before you go on?
　　☐ Yes ☐ No
　　Does it need batteries or charging?
　　☐ Yes ☐ No
　　Do you know how to turn it on/off and adjust volume?
　　☐ Yes ☐ No

You have been given instructions on how:
　　☐ To wear the microphone.
　　☐ To turn the microphone on and off.
　　☐ To change batteries if needed.
　　☐ To adjust the microphone volume.

You have found your presentation room and know when it will be available for early viewing.
　　Room number:
　　Availability:
　　Location:
　　Where is the closest restroom?
　　Where are the locations of alternate restrooms? _____

POWEREDGUIDE 6: WHO AM I?

Your name (and affiliation if relevant), and how to pronounce it if necessary.

Other employment history (if relevant)...

What is your knowledge/qualifications related to the topic you will be presenting?

What do you hope to accomplish during your presentation?

Where can the audience see, meet, text, or e-mail you after the presentation if they have or think of any questions or if they want to discuss any points?

POWEREDGUIDE 7: MEETING THE AUDIENCE

Questions to ask individual audience members:

What is your name?

Where are you from?

Where is that relative to where you are located? (If you are new to the area.)

What type of work do you do?

What made you decide to come to this presentation?

What kind of information do you hope I cover during my presentation?

Have you been to this conference/meeting/venue before?

POWEREDGUIDE 8: REDUCING ANXIETY CHECKLIST

☐ I know that I will have some jitters because all professions do.

☐ I know what is on this PoweredGuide but will review it anyway!

☐ I have filled out *PoweredGuide 1: Audience Analysis* and have a good idea about the likes, dislikes, and general makeup of my audience.

☐ I have looked over the room I will present in and have used *PoweredGuide 5: Arrival Checklist* to help me.

☐ I know where the closest restroom and an alternate restroom are located.

☐ My material is well organized and I am confident I know what I am going to say.

☐ I have rehearsed my presentation many times and know what expressions and gestures I will try to use and when I should insert pauses into the presentation.

☐ I have had friends watch and critique my presentation. I have incorporated any of their comments or ideas into subsequent rehearsals.

☐ I have reviewed *PoweredGuide 4: Your Prep Bag* and am ready for my presentation.

☐ I have practiced focused, deep breathing to help induce a relaxation response.

☐ I have practiced focusing on relaxing.

☐ I have practiced releasing tension with isometric exercises.

☐ I know that my PowerPoint bullets are the essence of my presentation and even if I forget to say something, my audience will have the information I wanted to get across.

☐ I will maintain eye contact with my audience members and will remember the three to five second eye contact rule.

☐ I have monitored my liquid consumption so as not to have an 'emergency'. I was especially aware of caffeinated drinks and alcohol.

☐ I have monitored my food consumption, being careful to avoid cholesterol, fat, and overly salty foods.

☐ I have monitored any medications I am on and will adjust them accordingly along with and snacks or liquids I might need.

☐ While waiting to go on I will repeat "I have got this! I have got this! I have got this!" in my head and know that I do have this!

☐ I know I have this and will knock this presentation out of the park!!

POWEREDGUIDE 9:
REHEARSAL CHECKLIST AND
COMMENTS

Thank you for spending some of your valuable time with me to give me honest feedback on my presentation. Please don't be afraid to be brutally honest. Better for me to know your true reaction here rather than in front of an audience when it might be too late.

I will provide a few notes about my audience.

Organization:
    Make-up of audience:
    Additional important information:

What did you think of my introduction?
    (0 is poor.)
    0 - 1 - 2 - 3 - 4 - 5 - 6 - 7 - 8 - 9 - 10
    Comments:

Would it give you a reason to listen if you were a member of the target audience?

Was there an 'attention grabber'?
    □ Yes □ No

Did you get an idea of what I was going to cover during the presentation?

☐ Yes ☐ No

What problems did you see in my introduction and how could I improve it?

Did there seem to be a logical progression or sequence in the flow of the presentation?

☐ Yes ☐ No

Comments:

What did you think of my overall delivery?

Did I speak loud enough?

☐ Yes ☐ No

Did I seem interested in the subject?

(0 is not interested at all.)

0 - 1 - 2 - 3 - 4 - 5 - 6 - 7 - 8 - 9 - 10

Did I have any disturbing mannerisms (fidgeting, twisting ring, etc.)?

☐ Yes ☐ No

Comment/examples:

Did I use distracting filler words (um, ah, OK, all set, etc.)?

☐ Yes ☐ No

Comment/examples:

Did I seem interested in the audience?

☐ Yes ☐ No

Did I speak too slowly or too quickly?

☐ Yes ☐ No

Comment/examples:

Did I speak clearly?
  ☐ Yes ☐ No
  Comments:

How was my questioning technique?
  (0 is poor.)
  0 - 1 - 2 - 3 - 4 - 5 - 6 - 7 - 8 - 9 - 10
  Comments:

Was the PowerPoint easy to read?
  ☐ Yes ☐ No

Would you make any changes to the PowerPoint if you were presenting?
  ☐ Yes ☐ No

How would you— should I— change it?

Did the conclusion sum up the presentation?
  ☐ Yes ☐ No
  Comments:

Was I dressed appropriately for the presentation?
  ☐ Yes ☐ No

The goal of my presentation was:

How successful do you think I was in reaching this goal?
  (0 is not successful.)
  0 - 1 - 2 - 3 - 4 - 5 - 6 - 7 - 8 - 9 - 10

Do you have any additional comments or criticisms (please be honest)?

Thank you for participating in my presentation rehearsal. If you can think of anything else you might want to comment about or expand on, please email, call or text me.

POWEREDGUIDE 10: TIME TO REVIEW YOUR PRESENTATION

Rate this presentation from 0–10 with 10 being outstanding.
0 - 1 - 2 - 3 - 4 - 5 - 6 - 7 - 8 - 9 - 10

Why did you rate your presentation like this?

How did you feel after your presentation?
(0 is not at all.)

Happy
0 - 1 - 2 - 3 - 4 - 5 - 6 - 7 - 8 - 9 - 10

Relieved
0 - 1 - 2 - 3 - 4 - 5 - 6 - 7 - 8 - 9 - 10

Accomplished
0 - 1 - 2 - 3 - 4 - 5 - 6 - 7 - 8 - 9 - 10

Frustrated
0 - 1 - 2 - 3 - 4 - 5 - 6 - 7 - 8 - 9 - 10

Embarrassed
0 - 1 - 2 - 3 - 4 - 5 - 6 - 7 - 8 - 9 - 10

What do you *feel* went right in your presentation?

What do you *feel* went wrong with your presentation?

What should you have done beforehand so this (these) problem(s) did not come up?

What will you do next time so this (these) problem(s) will not appear again?

If you received audience ratings or review sheets, what positive comments did they contain?

If you received audience ratings or review sheets, what negative comments did they contain?

What should you do to increase your audience ratings in future presentations?

What did you leave out or forget to say in your presentation?

Why did you leave it out or forget to say it?

What information should you have added to your presentation?

Why didn't you add it in the first place?

What changes should you make to this or your next presentation *slide show*?

What changes should you make to this or your next presentation *handouts*?

How was your timing?

If there was a timing problem, what steps should you take to improve your timing next time?

What did you leave out of your prep bag?

How accurate was your audience analysis?
    (0 is not accurate.)
    0 - 1 - 2 - 3 - 4 - 5 - 6 - 7 - 8 - 9 - 10

Why did you rate your audience analysis like this?

How can you do a better audience analysis next time?

What problems did you have with the presentation room?

Is there anything you should do or check to prevent problems like these from happening next time you present?

What types of questions did the audience ask?

Were these the types of questions you expected?

Why did they ask these questions? (Poor explanation, missed explanation? Poor audience analysis, etc.)

How can you prepare for questions next time you present?

Rate your nervousness.
    (0 is not nervous at all.)
    0 - 1 - 2 - 3 - 4 - 5 - 6 - 7 - 8 - 9 - 10

What steps did you take to reduce your nervousness?

What should you do next time to reduce your nervousness?

POWEREDGUIDE 11: VIRTUAL PRESENTATION OR MEETING PREP SHEET

How confident are you that you know how to use the virtual platform?

> (0 being no knowledge of the platform).
>
> 0 - 1 - 2 - 3 - 4 - 5 - 6 - 7 - 8 - 9 - 10
>
> *(You want to rate yourself at least a 9 or 10!)*

How confident are you that you know the wants, needs, and makeup of your audience? Refer to *PoweredGuide 1: Audience Analysis*.

> (0 being no knowledge of the audience.)
>
> 0 - 1 - 2 - 3 - 4 - 5 - 6 - 7 - 8 - 9 - 10
>
> *(You want to rate yourself at least a 9 or 10!)*

What techniques have you placed in your presentation to help hold your audience's attention?

> ☐ Questions
>
> ☐ Game playing
>
> ☐ Problem-solving
>
> ☐ Taking a poll
>
> ☐ Surveying the audience members
>
> ☐ Other (Please list):

How confident are you that these techniques will hold your audience's attention?

(0 being they will not hold attention.)

0 - 1 - 2 - 3 - 4 - 5 - 6 - 7 - 8 - 9 - 10

(You want to rate yourself at least a 9 or 10!)

You have rehearsed your presentation several times.

☐ Yes ☐ No

You have had a friend or friends sit through your presentation either live or recorded.

☐ Yes ☐ No

Your friend or friends made the following comments about your presentation:

You are going to do the following to remedy any negative comments they made:

What are the top three things you are worried about concerning your presentation or meeting?

1.
2.
3.

How are you going to change the above to your benefit?

1.
2.
3.

What problems do you foresee with the background area as you speak? How are you going to alleviate these problems?

Are there any lighting problems and how will you alleviate them?

How will you make sure that you are not disturbed or distracted by people, pets, outside noise, and/or equipment?

What will you be wearing for your presentation or meeting?

CPSIA information can be obtained
at www.ICGtesting.com
Printed in the USA
LVHW090607090421
683977LV00007B/221

9 780999 482902